"I cannot too strongly celebrate the publication of this book. Owing in part to several decades of dispute over justification and how a person is set right with God, we have tended to neglect another component of conversion no less important. Conversion under the terms of the new covenant is more than a matter of position and status in Christ, though never less: it includes miraculous Spirit-given transformation, something immeasurably beyond mere human resolution. It is new birth; it makes us new creatures; it demonstrates that the gospel is the power of God unto salvation. All the creedal orthodoxy in the world cannot replace it. The reason why 'You must be born again' is so important is that you must be born again."

D. A. Carson,
Trinity Evangelical Divinity School, Deerfield, Illinois

"Many will be thankful that John Piper is here addressing the key need of our times. Every awakening begins with the renewed discovery of Christ's teaching on the new birth. Here is that amazing teaching in lucid yet comprehensive form; with a relevance to readers worldwide."

Iain H. Murray

"When I was a boy my grandmother asked me, 'Have you been born again?' Though I didn't understand what she meant at the time, that question led to my conversion to Christ. In this wonderful book, Pastor John Piper rescues the term 'born again' from the abuse and overuse to which it is subject in our culture today. This is a fresh presentation of the evangelical doctrine of the new birth, a work filled with theological insight and pastoral wisdom."

Timothy George,
Beeson Divinity School, Samford University, Birmingham, Alabama
and Senior Editor of *Christianity Today*

"Expository and practical, this rich survey of New Testament teaching explores the nature of the new birth and the life which flows from it. Full of refreshment and encouragement, it reveals more deeply the glory of Christ and the gospel and motivates a renewed commitment to live out this good news and share it with others."

David Jackman,
The Proclamation Trust, London, U.K.

"The *doctrine* of the new birth is cheapened and hidden because so many 'professing Christians' have not experienced the *reality* of the new birth. The *reality* of the new birth is seemingly so little celebrated because so few understand the majestic *doctrine* of the new birth. *Finally Alive* sweeps away so much confusion and gives its readers so much cause for rejoicing in the saving work of God through Jesus Christ His beloved Son. Nothing could be more vital than God's people understanding what regeneration looks and feels and tastes and desires and speaks and walks and thinks like. Nothing could be more eternally important than Christian people knowing what the Bible teaches about the new birth and knowing that they have experienced it. One wonders why it's taken so long for a book on the new birth to be written! But now it has and I pray every reader rejoices in God for the rich beauties of Christ Jesus so compellingly shared in its pages."

Thabiti Anyabwile,
First Baptist Church, Grand Cayman, Cayman Islands

"John Piper rescues the term 'born again' from its contemporary status as a gauche or glib cliché and reunites it with a fully orbed biblical understanding of the new birth. Theologically thorough and yet heart-warmingly pastoral and practical, this important book should help God's people to value the remarkable status and responsibility of being 'born again.'"

Richard Cunningham,
Universities and Colleges Christian Fellowship (UCCF), U.K.

"Regeneration, or new birth, meaning simply the new you through, with, in, and under Christ, is a largely neglected theme today, but this fine set of sermons, criss-crossing the New Testament data with great precision, goes far to fill the gap. Highly recommended."

J .I. Packer,
Regent College, Vancouver, Canada

"The evangelical church is witnessing a resurgent commitment to social action—the doing of good deeds for a needy culture and world. While correct and commendable for many reasons, one danger now as ever is that 'good deeds' will supplant 'good news.' We need constant reminders of the truth of what Jesus said: 'What will it profit a man if he gains the whole world and forfeits his life?' (Matt. 16:26). John Piper's *Finally Alive* is a vivid and stirring description of the Bible's teaching on what it means to be born again. The good news of the gospel—that by God's grace, and through faith in Christ and the all-sufficiency of his atoning death, one may be fully forgiven and born again to newness of life that will never end—is a message that must be understood, believed, embraced, and proclaimed for true transformation of life to occur. 'You must be born again' (John 3:7) is a 'must' we dare not lose. *Finally Alive* unpacks the truth, the necessity, and the process of the new birth clearly and beautifully. For those curious about the Christian faith to those deeply committed to Christ and his ways, come read and behold the glory of any and every sinner's only hope—the miracle of the new birth that brings forth new life in Christ that will never end."

Bruce Ware,
The Southern Baptist Theological Seminary, Louisville, Kentucky

"*Have I been born again?* is not a question to be answered hastily. In this book, Piper strips away our complacency, arguing that many people falsely believe they are Christians. Because no issue could be more critical, I believe this is the most important book Piper has written."

Adrian Warnock
blogger

FINALLY ALIVE

What Happens When We Are Born Again

John Piper

CHRISTIAN
FOCUS

John Piper is pastor for Preaching at Bethlehem Baptist Church in Minneapolis, Minnesota. He has ministered at Bethlehem since 1980. John and his wife, Noël, have four sons, one daughter, and an increasing number of grandchildren.

Unless otherwise indicated Scripture quotations are from *The Holy Bible, English Standard Version*, copyright © 2001 by Crossway Bibles, a division of Good News Publishers. Used by permission. All rights reserved.

Scripture quotations marked KJV are taken from the *King James Version* of the Holy Bible.

© The Desiring God Foundation 2009

ISBN 978-1-84550-421-2

10 9 8 7 6 5 4 3 2 1

Published in 2009
by
Christian Focus Publications Ltd.,
Geanies House, Fearn, Ross-shire,
IV20 1TW, Scotland, Great Britain
www.christianfocus.com
and
Desiring God,
PO Box 2901 Minneapolis, Minnesota 55402, USA
www.desiringGod.org

Cover design by moose77.com
Printed in the Bell & Bain, Glasgow

Contents

Do not marvel that I said to you, "You must be born again." The wind blows where it wishes, and you hear its sound, but you do not know where it comes from or where it goes. So it is with everyone who is born of the Spirit.

John 3:7–8

INTRODUCTION

AUGUSTINE, LEWIS, BARNA,
AND THE BIBLE

The declaration of Jesus that we must be born again (John 3:7) is either deluded or devastating to the one who would be captain of his soul. Not many biblical realities are better designed by God to reveal our helplessness in sin. "The wind blows where it wishes, and you hear its sound, but you do not know where it comes from or where it goes. So it is with everyone who is born of the Spirit" (John 3:8). It is the Wind, not we, who finally rules the soul.

Two stories about the freedom of God's Spirit in the new birth will help us avoid superficial stereotypes about how he works. St. Augustine was converted to Christ in A. D. 386, and C. S. Lewis became a Christian in 1931. For both, it was after long struggles with unbelief. But the way the Wind blew with its final converting power was dramatically different for each.

AUGUSTINE'S STORY

For Augustine, the idol that kept him from Christ was sex. He had given way to his passions for the last sixteen years. He had left home at age sixteen, but his mother Monica had never ceased to pray. He was now almost thirty-two. "I began to search for a means of gaining the strength I needed to enjoy you [O Lord], but I could not find this means until I embraced the mediator between God and men, Jesus Christ."[1]

Then came one of the most important days in church history. It was late August, 386. Augustine was almost thirty-two years old. With his best friend Alypius, he was talking about the remarkable sacrifice and holiness of Antony, an Egyptian monk. Augustine was stung by his own bestial bondage to lust, when others were free and holy in Christ.

> There was a small garden attached to the house where we lodged....I now found myself driven by the tumult in my breast to take refuge in this garden, where no one could interrupt that fierce struggle in which I was my own contestant....I was beside myself with madness that would bring me sanity. I was dying a death that would bring me life....I was frantic, overcome by violent anger with myself for not accepting your will and entering into your covenant....I tore my hair and hammered my forehead with my fists; I locked my fingers and hugged my knees.[2]

But he began to see more clearly that the gain was far greater than the loss, and by a miracle of grace he began to see the beauty of chastity in the presence of Christ. The battle came down to the beauty of continence in fellowship with Christ versus the "trifles" that plucked at his flesh.

> I flung myself down beneath a fig tree and gave way to the tears which now streamed from my eyes....All at once I heard the singsong voice of a child in a nearby house. Whether it was the voice of a boy or a girl I cannot say, but

---

1 Aurelius Augustine, *Confessions*, 152 (VII, 18).
2 Ibid., 170–171 (VIII, 8).

again and again it repeated the refrain "Take it and read, take it and read."[3]

So I hurried back to the place where Alypius was sitting… seized [the book of Paul's epistles] and opened it, and in silence I read the first passage on which my eyes fell: "Not in reveling in drunkenness, not in lust and wantonness, not in quarrels and rivalries. Rather, arm yourselves with the Lord Jesus Christ; spend no more thought on nature and nature's appetites" (Rom. 13:13-14). I had no wish to read more and no need to do so. For in an instant, as I came to the end of the sentence, it was as though the light of confidence flooded into my heart and all the darkness of doubt was dispelled.[4]

Augustine was born again. He never turned back to the old ways. The Wind blew in a garden. It blew with a child's voice. It blew through a word of Scripture. And the darkness of his heart was dispelled.

LEWIS'S STORY

Since 1925, Lewis had been a Fellow of Magdalen College, Oxford, where he served as tutor in English Language and Literature. Lewis is perhaps best known today as the author of *The Chronicles of Narnia*.

On an evening in September, 1931, Lewis discussed Christianity with J. R. R. Tolkien (author of *The Lord of the Rings*) and with Hugo Dyson. In retrospect, we can say that God was putting things in place for the conversion that would follow the next day.

However, unlike Augustine, the conversion was unemotional and without manifest struggle. All the struggle had gone before. Here is how he tells the story of his saving bus ride to the zoo:

3 Ibid., 177–178 (VIII, 12).
4 Ibid., 178 (VIII, 12).

I know very well when, but hardly how, the final step was taken. I was driven into Whipsnade one sunny morning. When we set out I did not believe that Jesus Christ is the Son of God, and when we reached the zoo I did. And yet I had not exactly spent the journey in thought. Nor in great emotion. "Emotional" is perhaps the last word we can apply to some of the most important events. It was more like when a man, after long sleep, still lying motionless in bed, becomes aware that he is now awake. And it was, like that moment on top of the bus, ambiguous. Freedom, or necessity? Or do they differ at their maximum?[5]

Whether one is driven almost to madness in the moment of the new birth, or experiences it quietly on a bus to the zoo, the reality is in fact stupendous. Nothing is more important for two human souls than to say truly, "We know that we have passed out of death into life" (1 John 3:14). That's the reality this book is about.

THE DEFAMATION OF THE TERM BORN AGAIN

But not everyone today is jealous to esteem this miracle for the wonder that it is. If you go to research groups online, you can read things like this: "Born Again Christians Just as Likely to Divorce as Are Non-Christians." The same kind of statistics are given by Ron Sider in his book *The Scandal of the Evangelical Conscience: Why Are Christians Living Just Like the Rest of the World?* (Grand Rapids: Baker, 2005) and by Mark Regnerus in his book *Forbidden Fruit: Sex and Religion in the Lives of American Teenagers* (Oxford University Press, 2007).

What matters most for our concern in this book is the way the term *born again* is being used. In particular, the Barna Group, a Christian research firm, has used it in reporting their

5 C. S. Lewis, *Surprised by Joy: The Shape of My Early Life* (New York: Harcourt Brace and World Inc., 1955), 237.

findings. In the report titled "Born Again Christians Just as Likely to Divorce as Are Non-Christians," Barna uses the word *evangelicals* interchangeably with *born again* and reports that:

· Only nine percent of evangelicals tithe.
· Of 12,000 teenagers who took the pledge to wait for marriage, 80% had sex outside marriage in the next seven years.
· Twenty-six percent of traditional evangelicals do not think premarital sex is wrong.
· White evangelicals are more likely than Catholics and mainline Protestants to object to having black neighbors.[6]

In other words, the broadly defined evangelical church as a whole in America and the West in general is apparently not very unlike the world. It goes to church on Sunday and has a veneer of religion, but its religion is basically an add-on to the same way of life the world lives, not a transforming power.

A PROFOUND MISTAKE

I want to say loud and clear that when the Barna Group uses the term *born again* to describe American church-goers whose lives are indistinguishable from the world, and who sin as much as the world, and sacrifice for others as little as the world, and embrace injustice as readily as the world, and covet things as greedily as the world, and enjoy God-ignoring entertainment as enthusiastically as the world—when the term *born again* is used to describe these professing Christians, the Barna Group is making a profound mistake. It is using the biblical term *born again* in a way that would make it unrecognizable by Jesus and the biblical writers.

6 Statistics reported in Ron Sider, *The Scandal of the Evangelical Conscience* (Grand Rapids, MI: Baker Books, 2005), 18–28.

Here is the way the researchers defined *born again* in their research:

> "Born again Christians" were defined in these surveys as people who said they have made "a personal commitment to Jesus Christ that is still important in their life today" and who also indicated they believe that when they die they will go to Heaven because they had confessed their sins and had accepted Jesus Christ as their savior. Respondents were not asked to describe themselves as "born again." Being classified as "born again" is not dependent upon church or denominational affiliation or involvement.[7]

In other words, in this research the term *born again* refers to people who *say* things. They say, "I have a personal commitment to Jesus Christ. It's important to me." They say, "I believe that I will go to Heaven when I die. I have confessed my sins and accepted Jesus Christ as my Savior." Then the Barna Group takes them at their word, ascribes to them the infinitely important reality of the new birth, and then slanders that precious biblical reality by saying that regenerate hearts have no more victory over sin than unregenerate hearts.

THE NEW TESTAMENT
MOVES IN THE OPPOSITE DIRECTION

I'm not saying their research is wrong. It appears to be appallingly right. I am not saying that the church is not as worldly as they say it is. *I am* saying that the writers of the New Testament think in exactly the opposite direction about being born again. Instead of moving from a profession of faith, to the label *born again*, to the worldliness of these so-called *born again* people, to the conclusion that the new birth does

---

7 www.barna.org/FlexPage.aspx?Page=BarnaUpdate&BarnaUpdateID=170, accessed 05-05-08.

not radically change people, the New Testament moves in the other direction.

It moves from the absolute certainty that the new birth radically changes people, to the observation that many professing Christians are indeed (as the Barna Group says) not radically changed, to the conclusion that they are not born again. The New Testament, unlike the Barna Group, does not defile the new birth with the worldliness of unregenerate, professing Christians.

For example, one of the main points of the First Epistle of John is to drive home this very truth:

· 1 John 2:29: "If you know that he is righteous, you may be sure that everyone who practices righteousness has been born of him."
· 1 John 3:9: "No one born of God makes a practice of sinning, for God's seed abides in him, and he cannot keep on sinning because he has been born of God."
· 1 John 4:7: "Beloved, let us love one another, for love is from God, and whoever loves has been born of God and knows God."
· 1 John 5:4: "Everyone who has been born of God overcomes the world. And this is the victory that has overcome the world—our faith."
· 1 John 5:18: "We know that everyone who has been born of God does not keep on sinning, but he who was born of God protects him, and the evil one does not touch him."

We will come back to texts like these in the chapters to come. There are many questions to answer, and we will distance ourselves plainly from perfectionism and deal realistically with the failures of genuine Christians.

But for now, is it not true that these statements appear to be written with the very claims of the Barna Group in mind? Are these texts not addressed to the false claim that born again people are morally indistinguishable from the world? The Bible is profoundly aware of such people in the church. That is one reason why 1 John was written. But instead of following the Barna Group, the Bible says that the research is not finding that born again people are permeated with worldliness; the research is finding that the church is permeated by people who are not born again.

"Regeneration"

This is a book about the new birth. What does the Bible teach about being born again? Another word for being born again is *regeneration*. It is helpful to use that word from time to time. I hope you are willing to add it to your vocabulary if it's not there. That would include adding the word *regenerate* as both a verb (God *regenerates* people) and an adjective (only *regenerate* people are saved). Regenerate people and born again people are the same. I will use the terms interchangeably.

Desecrating the Term *Born Again*

In this introduction, I will give an overview of where we are going and why. You can already see one of the reasons I want to focus on this issue. The term *born again* is desecrated when it is used the way the Barna Group uses it. And, of course, that particular misuse of the biblical term is not the only kind.

The term *born again* has come to mean for many people merely that someone or something got a new lease on life. So a quick survey of the internet shows that Cisco Systems, the communications company, has been born again; and the Green Movement has been born again; the Davie Shipyard in Montreal has been born again; the west end in Boston has been born again; Kosher foods for Orthodox Jews have been born again, and so on. So it's not surprising that we have to be careful when we read that 45% of Americans say they have been religiously born again.

The term *born again* is very precious and very crucial in the Bible. So our main concern is to know what God intends when the Bible uses this language, so that by his grace we may experience it and help others do the same. It is of enormous consequence that we know what being born again really means.

WHAT REALLY HAPPENED TO US?

Another reason for a book on the new birth is to help followers of Christ to know what really happened to us when we were converted. It is far more glorious than many think it is. It is also more glorious than I think it is. It is wonderful beyond all human comprehension. But that mystery is not because there is little about it in the Bible. There is much about it in the Bible. It's because when all is understood as well as we can understand it in this age when we see "in a mirror dimly" (1 Cor. 13:12), there is still more. So I hope that when we are done, we will know more fully and know more accurately what happened to us when we were born again.

WHAT MUST HAPPEN TO BE BORN AGAIN

Another reason for this treatment of the new birth is that there are millions of people who do not yet follow Christ. They are not born again. I pray that God might use this book as one means of their new birth. Some of them are church attenders and church members, even leaders. But they are not born again. They are cultural Christians. Religion is a formal, external thing. There has been no true inner awakening from spiritual death to spiritual life.

I want to serve those people by showing them what must happen to them. And by the word and the prayers of believers and the Spirit of God, I hope that this book will be a means of many being born again. The new birth, as we will see, is not a work of man. No human makes the new birth happen. No preacher and no writer can make it happen. You can't make it happen to yourself. God makes it happen. It happens to us, not by us.

But it always happens through the word of God. Here is the way the apostle Peter puts it: "Since you have been born again, not of perishable seed but of imperishable, through the living and abiding word of God....And this word is the good news that was preached to you" (1 Pet. 1:23–25). So even though God is the one who begets his children, the seed by which he does it is the word of God, the gospel that we preach. So I pray that one of the great effects of these very human chapters will be that very supernatural miracle. My aim is to explain the new birth as clearly as I can from the Bible so that readers can see it for themselves.

There are three reasons I want you who are Christians to know what happened to you when you were born again:

1 When you are truly born again and grow in the grace and knowledge of what the Lord has done for you, your fellowship with God will be sweet, and your assurance that he is your Father will be deep. I want that for you.
2 If you know what really happened to you in your new birth, you will treasure God and his Spirit and his Son and his word more highly than you ever have. In this, Christ will be glorified.
3 In the process of believers discovering what really happened to them, the seriousness and the supernatural nature of conversion will rise and that, I pray, will serve a more general awakening of authenticity in the Christian church so that religious hypocrisy will diminish and the world will see real love and sacrifice and courage in the service of Christ.

CRUCIAL QUESTIONS ABOUT BEING *BORN AGAIN*

There are several crucial questions we will be asking. One is: *What is the new birth?* That is, what actually happens? What is it like? What changes? What comes into being that wasn't there before?

Along the way, we will be trying to explain how the new birth relates to other things that God does to save us. For example, how does being born again relate to:

· God's effectual calling ("Those whom he called he justified," Rom. 8:30),
· the new creation ("If anyone is in Christ, he is a new creation," 2 Cor. 5:17),
· God's drawing us to Christ ("No one can come to me unless the Father who sent me draws him," John 6:44),
· God's giving people to his Son ("All that the Father gives me will come to me," John 6:37),
· God's opening our hearts ("The Lord opened her heart to pay attention to what was said by Paul," Acts 16:14),
· God's illumining our hearts ("God...has shone in our hearts to give the light of the knowledge of the glory of God in the face of Jesus Christ," 2 Cor. 4:6),
· God's taking the heart of stone out and giving us a heart of flesh ("I will remove the heart of stone from your flesh and give you a heart of flesh," Ezek. 36:26),
· God's making us alive ("even when we were dead in our trespasses, [God] made us alive together with Christ," Eph. 2:5),
· God's adopting us into his family ("You have received the Spirit of adoption as sons, by whom we cry, 'Abba! Father!'" Rom. 8:15).

How does God's act of regeneration relate to all these wonderful ways of describing what happened to us when God saved us?

Another question we will ask is: *Why is the new birth necessary?* Jesus said to Nicodemus in John 3:7, "You must be born again." Not "I suggest it," or "Your life would improve if you added this experience." Why is it that "unless one is born again he cannot see the kingdom of God" (John 3:3)? This is one of the great reasons for pursuing a right knowledge of the new birth. Until we realize that we must be born again, and why we must be born again, we probably will not realize what our condition really is without salvation.

Most people do not know what is really wrong with them. One way to help them make a true and terrible and hopeful diagnosis is to show them the kind of remedy God has provided, namely, the new birth. If you have a sore on your ankle and after the doctor does his test, he comes in and says, "I have hard news: We have to take your leg off just below the knee," then that remedy tells you more about the sore than many erudite medical words. So it is with the remedy "You must be born again."

After *What?* and *Why?* we will ask *How?* How does it come about? What does God do in regeneration? What did he do in history to make it possible? If new birth is decisively the work of God, which it is, how do I experience it? Is there anything I can do to make it happen? What is my part in bringing it about?

After *What?* and *Why?* and *How?* we ask *For what?* What is the aim of the new birth? What effects does it have? What changes come about in life? What is it like to live as a born-again person?

And finally, *What can we do to help others be born again?* If God is the great Doer in this affair, what can we do? Does our doing really matter? We will end with the practical matter of personal evangelism and how it relates to the new birth.

THE GREAT NEED AND THE USE OF MEANS

Much is at stake in seeing the new birth in true biblical proportions. Heaven and hell are at stake—and a church in the world *now* that acts more like Jesus and less like the culture around it.

Which brings us back to where we started, namely, the claim that born again Christians have lifestyles of worldliness and sin that are indistinguishable from the unregenerate. I don't think so. 1 John 5:4: "Everyone who has been born of God overcomes the world. And this is the victory that has overcome the world— our faith." But my conviction is not rosy news for the church. It implies that there are millions of church attenders who are not born again.

Nevertheless, in spite of this conviction, I will distance myself from perfectionism. In other words, I don't think that the new birth makes us perfect in this life. Sin remains, and the fight of faith is a daily necessity. Some unbelievers look like better people than some believers. But that is because some pretty bad people have been born again, and the process of transformation is not always as fast as we would like.

It's also because there are unregenerate people who for all kinds of genetic and social reasons conform to an outward morality while being God-indifferent or God-hostile on the inside. God sees the line between the regenerate and the unregenerate perfectly. We don't. But there is such a line, and those who have been born again are being changed, even if slowly, from one degree of humility and love to the next.

This matters. It matters for eternity, and it matters for the glory of Christ in this life. If people are to enter finally into the kingdom of God (John 3:3), and if the church is to let her light shine on earth that people may give glory to God (Matt. 5:16), then the new birth must be experienced.

God is the great Doer in this miracle of regeneration. And he has not been silent about it. This means that he does not want us to be ignorant of what he does in the new birth. It means that knowing what he has revealed about the new birth is good for us. When Jesus said to Nicodemus, "You must be born again" (John 3:7), he was not sharing interesting and unimportant information. He was leading him to eternal life.

That's what I hope this echo of Jesus' words—this book—will do. Only God regenerates human beings. But he uses means. May his mercy make this one of them. If he does that for you (or if he already has), then you are (or you will be) truly, invincibly, finally alive.

PART ONE
WHAT IS THE NEW BIRTH?

Now there was a man of the Pharisees named Nicodemus, a ruler of the Jews. This man came to Jesus by night and said to him, "Rabbi, we know that you are a teacher come from God, for no one can do these signs that you do unless God is with him." Jesus answered him, "Truly, truly, I say to you, unless one is born again he cannot see the kingdom of God." Nicodemus said to him, "How can a man be born when he is old? Can he enter a second time into his mother's womb and be born?" Jesus answered, "Truly, truly, I say to you, unless one is born of water and the Spirit, he cannot enter the kingdom of God. That which is born of the flesh is flesh, and that which is born of the Spirit is spirit. Do not marvel that I said to you, 'You must be born again.' The wind blows where it wishes, and you hear its sound, but you do not know where it comes from or where it goes. So it is with everyone who is born of the Spirit." Nicodemus said to him, "How can these things be?" Jesus answered him, "Are you the teacher of Israel and yet you do not understand these things?"

John 3:1–10

I

The Supernatural Creation
of Spiritual Life

Jesus said to Nicodemus in John 3:3, "Truly, truly, I say to you, unless one is born again he cannot see the kingdom of God." He was speaking to all of us when he said that. Nicodemus was not a special case. You and I must be born again, or we will not see the kingdom of God. That means we will not be saved; we will not be part of God's family, and we will not go to heaven. Instead, we will go to hell if we are not born again. That's what Jesus says later in this chapter about the person who does not believe on Christ: "The wrath of God remains on him" (John 3:36). This is no joking matter. Jesus uses hard words for hard realities. That is what love does. The opposite is called pandering.

Nicodemus was one of the Pharisees, the most religious Jewish leaders. Jesus said to them in Matthew 23:15 and 33, "Woe to you, scribes and Pharisees, hypocrites! For you travel across sea and land to make a single proselyte, and when he becomes a proselyte, you make him twice as much a child of hell as yourselves....You serpents, you brood of vipers, how are you to escape being sentenced to hell?" So the topic of the new birth is not marginal. It is central. Eternity hangs in the balance when we are talking about the new birth. Unless one is born again, he cannot see the kingdom of God.

THE NEW BIRTH IS UNSETTLING

The question we are asking in this chapter is: *What happens in the new birth?* Before I try to answer that question, let me mention a very earnest concern that I have about the way these chapters will be read. I am aware that these chapters will be unsettling to many—just as the words of Jesus are unsettling to us again and again, if we take them seriously. There are at least three reasons for this.

First, Jesus' teaching about the new birth confronts us with our hopeless spiritual and moral and legal condition apart from God's regenerating grace. Before the new birth happens to us, we are *spiritually* dead; we are *morally* selfish and rebellious; and we are *legally* guilty before God's law and under his wrath. When Jesus tells us that we must be born again, he is telling us that our present condition is hopelessly unresponsive, corrupt, and guilty. Apart from amazing grace in our lives, we don't like to hear this assessment of ourselves, so it is unsettling when Jesus tells us that we must be born again.

Second, teaching about the new birth is unsettling because it refers to something that is done to us, not something we do. John 1:13 emphasizes this. It refers to the children of God as those "who were born, not of blood nor of the will of the flesh nor of the will of man, but of God." God causes the new birth; we don't. Peter stresses the same thing: "Blessed be the God and Father of our Lord Jesus Christ! According to his great mercy, he has caused us to be born again" (1 Pet. 1:3).

We do not cause the new birth. God causes the new birth. Any spiritually good thing that we do is a result of the new birth, not a cause of the new birth. This means that the new birth is taken out of our hands. It is not in our control. And so it confronts us with our helplessness and our absolute dependence on Someone outside ourselves. This is unsettling. We are told that we won't see the kingdom of God if we're not born again. And we're told that we can't make ourselves to be born again.

The third reason Jesus' teaching about the new birth is unsettling, therefore, is that it confronts us with the absolute freedom of God. Apart from God, we are spiritually dead in our selfishness and rebellion. We are by nature children of wrath (Eph. 2:3). Our rebellion is so deep that we cannot detect or desire the glory of Christ in the gospel (2 Cor. 4:4). Therefore, if we are going to be born again, it will rely decisively and ultimately on God. His decision to make us alive will not be a response to what we as spiritual corpses do, but what we do will be a response to his making us alive. For most people, at least at first, this is unsettling.

MY HOPE: STABILIZE AND SAVE, NOT JUST UNSETTLE

In view of how disturbing this can be to the tender conscience as well as the hard heart, I want to be very careful. I do not want to cause tender souls any unnecessary distress. And I do not want to give false hope to those who have confused morality or religion for spiritual life. Pray as you read this book that it will not have either of these destructive effects.

I feel like I am taking eternal souls in my hands. And yet I know that I have no power in myself to give them life. But God does. And I am very hopeful that he will do what he says in Ephesians 2:4–5: "But God, being rich in mercy, because of the great love with which he loved us, even when we were dead in our trespasses, made us alive together with Christ—by grace you have been saved." God loves to magnify the riches of his life-giving grace where Christ is lifted up in truth. That is my hope: that these chapters will not just unsettle but stabilize and save.

THE PLAN

So let's turn now to the question: *What happens in the new birth?* I will try to put the answer in three statements. The first two we will deal with in this chapter, and the third we deal with in the next: 1) What happens in the new birth is not getting new religion but getting new life. 2) What happens in the new birth is not merely affirming the supernatural in Jesus but experiencing the supernatural in yourself. 3) What happens in the new birth is not the improvement of your old human nature but the creation of a new human nature—a nature that is really *you*, and is forgiven and cleansed; and a nature that is really *new*, and is being formed by the indwelling Spirit of God. Let's take those one at a time.

NEW LIFE, NOT NEW RELIGION

What happens in the new birth is not getting new religion but getting new life. The first three verses of John 3 go like this:

> Now there was a man of the Pharisees named Nicodemus, a ruler of the Jews. This man came to Jesus by night and said to him, "Rabbi, we know that you are a teacher come from God, for no one can do these signs that you do unless God is with him." Jesus answered him, "Truly, truly, I say to you, unless one is born again he cannot see the kingdom of God."

John makes sure that we know that Nicodemus is a Pharisee and a ruler of the Jews. The Pharisees were the most rigorously religious of all the Jewish groups. To this one, Jesus says (in v. 3), "Truly, truly, I say to you, unless one is born again he cannot see the kingdom of God." Even more personally, he says in verse 7, "You must be born again." So one of John's points is: All of Nicodemus' religion, all of his amazing Pharisaic study and discipline and law-keeping, cannot replace the need for the new birth.

What Nicodemus needs, and what you and I need, is not religion but life. The point of referring to new birth is that birth brings a new life into the world.[8] In one sense, of course, Nicodemus is alive. He is breathing, thinking, feeling, acting. He is a human created in God's image. But evidently, Jesus thinks he's dead. There is no spiritual life in Nicodemus. Spiritually, he is unborn. He needs life, not more religious activities or more religious zeal. He has plenty of that.

Recall what Jesus said in Luke 9:60 to the man who wanted to put off following Jesus so he could bury his father. Jesus said, "Leave the dead to bury their own dead." That means there are physically dead people who need burying. And there are spiritually dead people who can bury them. In other words, Jesus thought in terms of people who walk around with much apparent life, but who are dead. In his parable about the prodigal son, the father says, "This my son was dead, and is alive again" (Luke 15:24).

Nicodemus did not need religion; he needed life—spiritual life. What happens in the new birth is that life comes into being

---

8 Throughout this book, we will not make any significant distinction between the imagery of conception and the imagery of birth. Even pre-scientific, first-century people knew that children were alive and kicking before birth. But the biblical writers did not press the details of gestation in discussing the new birth. In general, when they (and we) speak of the new birth, we are speaking more broadly of new life coming into being whether one thinks of the point of conception or the point of birth.

that was not there before. New life happens at new birth. This is not religious activity or discipline or decision. This is the coming into being of life. That's the first way of describing what happens in the new birth.

EXPERIENCING THE SUPERNATURAL, NOT JUST AFFIRMING IT

Second, what happens in the new birth is not merely affirming the supernatural in Jesus but experiencing the supernatural in yourself. Nicodemus says in verse 2, "Rabbi, we know that you are a teacher come from God, for no one can do these signs that you do unless God is with him." In other words, Nicodemus sees in Jesus' ministry a genuine divine activity. He admits that Jesus is from God. Jesus does the works of God. To this, Jesus does not respond by saying, "I wish everyone in Palestine could see the truth that you see about me." Instead, he says, "You must be born again, or you will never see the kingdom of God."

Seeing signs and wonders, and being amazed at them, and giving the miracle-worker credit for them that he is from God, saves nobody. This is one of the great dangers of signs and wonders: You don't need a new heart to be amazed at them. The old, fallen human nature is all that's needed to be amazed at signs and wonders. And the old, fallen human nature is willing to say that the miracle-worker is from God. The devil himself knows that Jesus is the Son of God and works miracles (Mark 1:24). No, Nicodemus, seeing Jesus as a miracle-worker sent from God is not the key to the kingdom of God. "Truly, truly, I say to you, unless one is born again he cannot see the kingdom of God."

In other words, what matters is not merely affirming the supernatural in Jesus but experiencing the supernatural in yourself. The new birth is supernatural, not natural. It cannot be accounted for by things that are already found in this world.

Verse 6 emphasizes the supernatural nature of the new birth: "That which is born of the flesh is flesh, and that which is born of the Spirit is spirit." The flesh is what we are naturally. The Spirit of God is the supernatural Person who brings about the new birth.

Jesus says this again in verse 8: "The wind blows where it wishes, and you hear its sound, but you do not know where it comes from or where it goes. So it is with everyone who is born of the Spirit." The Spirit is not a part of this natural world. He is above nature. He is supernatural. Indeed, he is God. He blows where he wills. We don't control him. He is free and sovereign. He is the immediate cause of the new birth.

So, Nicodemus, Jesus says, what happens in the new birth is not merely affirming the supernatural in me, but experiencing the supernatural in yourself. You must be born again. And not in a natural way (metaphorically speaking), but in a supernatural way. God the Holy Spirit must come into you and bring new life into existence.

In the next chapter, we will look at the words in verse 5: "Truly, truly, I say to you, unless one is born of water and the Spirit, he cannot enter the kingdom of God." What do water and Spirit refer to here? And how does that help us understand what is happening in the new birth?

JESUS IS THE LIFE WE RECEIVE AT NEW BIRTH

But in the space that remains in this chapter, I want to make a crucial connection between being born again by the Spirit and having eternal life through faith in Jesus. What we have seen so far is that what happens in the new birth is a supernatural work by the Holy Spirit to bring spiritual life into being where it did not exist. Jesus says it again in John 6:63: "It is the Spirit who gives life; the flesh is no help at all."

But the Gospel of John makes something else clear as well: Jesus himself is the life that the Holy Spirit gives. Or we could say: The spiritual life that he gives, he only gives in connection with Jesus. Union with Jesus is where we experience supernatural, spiritual life. Jesus said in John 14:6, "I am the way, and the truth, and the life. No one comes to the Father except through me." In John 6:35, he said, "I am the bread of life." And in John 20:31, the apostle says, "These are written so that you may believe that Jesus is the Christ, the Son of God, and that by believing you may have life in his name."

So there is no spiritual life—no eternal life—apart from connection with Jesus and belief in Jesus. We will have lots more to say about the relationship between the new birth and faith in Jesus. But we can put it this way for now: In the new birth, the Holy Spirit unites us to Christ in a living union. Christ is life. Christ is the vine where life flows. We are the branches (John 15:1–17). What happens in the new birth is the supernatural creation of new spiritual life, and it is created through union with Jesus Christ. The Holy Spirit brings us into vital connection with Christ who is the way, the truth, and the life. That is the objective reality of what happens in the new birth.

And from our side, the way we experience this is that faith in Jesus is awakened in our hearts. Spiritual life and faith in Jesus come into being together. The new life makes the faith possible, and since spiritual life always awakens faith and expresses itself in faith, there is no life without faith in Jesus. Therefore, we should never separate the new birth from faith in Jesus. From God's side, we are united to Christ in the new birth. That's what the Holy Spirit does. From our side, we experience this union by faith in Jesus.

NEVER SEPARATE THE NEW BIRTH AND FAITH IN JESUS

Here is how John puts them together in his First Epistle: "Everyone who has been *born of God* overcomes the world. And this is the victory that has overcome the world—our *faith*" (1 John 5:4). "Born of God" is the key to victory. "Faith" is the key to victory. Both are true because faith is the way we experience being born of God. Being born of God always brings faith with it. The life given in the new birth is the life of faith. The two are never separate.

Or consider how John says it in 1 John 5:11–12: "This is the testimony, that God gave us eternal life, and this life is in his Son. Whoever has the Son has life; whoever does not have the Son of God does not have life." Therefore, when Jesus says, "It is the Spirit who gives life" (John 6:63), and, "You must be born of the Spirit" (John 3:5, 8), and, "Believing you may have life" (John 20:31), he means: In the new birth, the Holy Spirit supernaturally gives us new spiritual life by connecting us with Jesus Christ through faith. For Jesus is life.

Therefore, when answering the question *What happens in the new birth?* never separate these two sayings of Jesus in John 3: "Unless one is born again he cannot see the kingdom of God" (v. 3), and, "Whoever believes in the Son has eternal life" (v. 36). What happens in the new birth is the creation of life in union with Christ. And part of how God does that is by the creation of faith, which is how we experience our union with Christ.

Now there was a man of the Pharisees named Nicodemus, a ruler of the Jews. This man came to Jesus by night and said to him, "Rabbi, we know that you are a teacher come from God, for no one can do these signs that you do unless God is with him." Jesus answered him, "Truly, truly, I say to you, unless one is born again he cannot see the kingdom of God." Nicodemus said to him, "How can a man be born when he is old? Can he enter a second time into his mother's womb and be born?" Jesus answered, "Truly, truly, I say to you, unless one is born of water and the Spirit, he cannot enter the kingdom of God. That which is born of the flesh is flesh, and that which is born of the Spirit is spirit. Do not marvel that I said to you, 'You must be born again.' The wind blows where it wishes, and you hear its sound, but you do not know where it comes from or where it goes. So it is with everyone who is born of the Spirit." Nicodemus said to him, "How can these things be?" Jesus answered him, "Are you the teacher of Israel and yet you do not understand these things?"

John 3:1–10

2

YOU ARE STILL YOU, BUT NEW

In this chapter, we will continue the answer to the question of Chapter 1, *What happens in the new birth?* Jesus said to Nicodemus in John 3:7, "Do not marvel that I said to you, 'You must be born again.'" In verse 3, he told Nicodemus—and us—that our eternal lives depend on being born again: "Truly, truly, I say to you, unless one is born again he cannot see the kingdom of God." So we are not dealing with something marginal or optional or cosmetic in the Christian life. The new birth is not like the make-up that morticians use to try to make corpses look more like they are alive. The new birth is the creation of spiritual life, not the imitation of life.

We began to answer the question *What happens in the new birth?* with two statements: 1) What happens in the new birth is not getting new religion but getting new life, and 2) What happens in the new birth is not merely affirming the supernatural in Jesus but experiencing the supernatural in yourself.

New Life through the Holy Spirit

Nicodemus was a Pharisee and had lots of religion. But he had no spiritual life. And he saw the supernatural work of God in Jesus, but he didn't experience the supernatural work of God in himself. So putting our two points together from Chapter 1, what Nicodemus needed was new spiritual life imparted supernaturally through the Holy Spirit. What makes the new life *spiritual* and what makes it *supernatural* is that it is the work of God the Spirit. It is something above the natural life of our physical hearts and brains.

In John 3:6, Jesus says, "That which is born of the flesh is flesh, and that which is born of the Spirit is spirit." The flesh does have a kind of life. Every human being is living flesh. But not every human being is living spirit. To be a living spirit, or to have spiritual life, Jesus says, we must be "born of the Spirit." Flesh gives rise to one kind of life. The Spirit gives rise to another kind of life. If we don't have this second kind, we will not see the kingdom of God.

By the Spirit, In Jesus

Then, as we came to the end of the previous chapter, we noticed two very important things: the relationship of the new birth to Jesus, and the relationship of the new birth to faith. Jesus said, "I am the way, and the truth, and the *life*" (John 14:6). The apostle John said, "God gave us eternal life, and this life is *in his Son*. Whoever has the Son has life; whoever does not have the Son of God does not have life" (1 John 5:11–12).

So on the one hand, the new life we need is "in the Son"— Jesus is that life. If you have him, you have new spiritual, eternal life. And on the other hand, in John 6:63, Jesus says, "It is the

Spirit who gives life." And unless you are born of the Spirit, you cannot enter the kingdom of God (John 3:5).

So we have life by being connected with the Son of God who is our life, and we have that life by the work of the Spirit. We concluded, therefore, that the work of the Spirit in regeneration is to impart new life to us by uniting us to Christ. The way John Calvin says it is: "The Holy Spirit is the bond by which Christ effectually unites us to himself."[9]

Then we saw the connection with faith in John 20:31: "These are written so that you may believe that Jesus is the Christ, the Son of God, and that by believing you may have life in his name." And we saw the connection in 1 John 5:4: "Everyone who has been born of God overcomes the world. And this is the victory that has overcome the world—our faith." So we summed up what we had seen like this: In the new birth, the Holy Spirit supernaturally gives us new spiritual life by connecting us with Jesus Christ through faith.

NEW CREATION, NOT IMPROVING THE OLD

Which brings us now to the third way of describing what happens in the new birth. What happens in the new birth is not the improvement of your old human nature but the creation of a new human nature—a nature that is really *you*, forgiven and cleansed; and a nature that is really *new*, being formed in you by the indwelling Spirit of God.

I'll take you with me on the short version of the trip I took to arrive at this observation. In John 3:5, Jesus says to Nicodemus, "Truly, truly, I say to you, unless one is born of water and the Spirit, he cannot enter the kingdom of God." What does Jesus mean by the two terms "by water and the Spirit"? Some

9 John Calvin, *Institutes of the Christian Religion* (Philadelphia: The Westminster Press, 1960), 538 (III, 1, 1).

denominations believe that this is a reference to water baptism as the way the Spirit unites us to Christ. For example, one website explains it like this:

> Holy Baptism is the basis of the whole Christian life, the gateway to life in the Spirit and the door which gives access to the other sacraments. Through Baptism we are freed from sin and reborn as sons of God; we become members of Christ, are incorporated into the Church, and made sharers in her mission: "Baptism is the sacrament of regeneration through water in the word."[10]

Millions of people have been taught that their baptism caused them to be born again. If this is not true, it is a great and global tragedy. I do not believe it is true. So what then does Jesus mean by the words "Unless one is born of water and the Spirit..."?

Why "Water" Is Not a Reference to Baptism

There are several reasons why I think the reference to water here is not a reference to Christian baptism.

First, if this were a reference to Christian baptism and it were as essential for new birth as some say it is, it seems strange that it drops out of view in the rest of this chapter as Jesus tells us how to have eternal life. Verse 15: "Whoever believes in him may have eternal life." Verse 16: "Whoever believes in him [will] not perish but have eternal life." Verse 18: "Whoever believes in him is not condemned." It would seem strange, if baptism were that essential, that it would not be mentioned along with faith in the rest of the chapter.

Second, the analogy with the wind in verse 8 would seem strange if being born again were so firmly attached to water baptism. Jesus says, "The wind blows where it wishes, and you hear its sound, but you do not know where it comes from or where

10 www.christusrex.org/www1/CDHN/baptism.html, accessed 04-30-08

it goes. So it is with everyone who is born of the Spirit." This seems to say that God is as free as the wind in causing regeneration. But if it happened every time a baby is sprinkled, that would not seem to be true. In that case, the wind would be very confined by the sacrament. It does not sound as if Jesus is thinking in sacramental or baptismal terms.

Third, if Jesus is referring to Christian baptism, it seems strange that he would say to Nicodemus, the Pharisee, in verse 10, "Are you the teacher of Israel and yet you do not understand these things?" That makes sense if Jesus is referring to something taught in the Old Testament, which Nicodemus should have known and applied. But if Jesus is referring to a Christian baptism that will come later, and get its meaning from the life and death of Jesus, it doesn't seem like he would have scolded Nicodemus that a teacher in Israel does not understand what he is saying.

Finally, that same statement in verse 10 sends us back to the Old Testament for some background, and what we find is that water and spirit are closely linked in the New Covenant promises, especially in Ezekiel 36. This text in Ezekiel is the basis for the rest of this chapter.

WATER AND SPIRIT IN EZEKIEL 36

Ezekiel is prophesying what God will do for his people when he brings them back from exile in Babylon. The implications are much larger than just for the people of Israel, because Jesus claims to secure the New Covenant by his blood for all who will trust in him (Luke 22:20). And Ezekiel 36:24–28 is one version of the New Covenant promises like the ones in Jeremiah 31:31–34.

> I will take you from the nations and gather you from all the countries and bring you into your own land. I will sprinkle clean water on you, and you shall be clean from

> all your uncleannesses, and from all your idols I will cleanse you. And I will give you a new heart, and a new spirit I will put within you. And I will remove the heart of stone from your flesh and give you a heart of flesh. And I will put my Spirit within you, and cause you to walk in my statutes and be careful to obey my rules. You shall dwell in the land that I gave to your fathers, and you shall be my people, and I will be your God. (Ezek. 36:24–28)

I think this is the passage that gives rise to Jesus words "Unless one is born of *water* and the *Spirit*, he cannot enter the kingdom of God." To whom does God say, "You shall be my people, and I will be your God" (v. 28)? Answer: To the ones to whom he says, "I will sprinkle clean *water* on you, and you shall be clean from all your uncleannesses" (v. 25); and verse 26: To the ones to whom he says, "I will give you a new heart, and a new *spirit* I will put within you." In other words, the ones who will "enter the kingdom" are those who have a newness that involves a *cleansing* of the old and a *creation* of the new.

So I conclude that "water and Spirit" in Ezekiel 36 refer to two aspects of our newness when we are born again. And the reason both are important is this: When we say that a new spirit (or a new heart) is given to us, we don't mean that we cease to be the human being—the morally accountable self—that we have always been. I was the individual human being John Piper before I was born again, and I have been the individual human being John Piper since I was born again. There is a continuity. That's why there has to be cleansing. If the old human being, John Piper, were completely obliterated, the whole concept of forgiveness and cleansing would be irrelevant. There would be nothing left over from the past to forgive or cleanse.

We know that the Bible tells us that our old self was crucified (Rom. 6:6), and that we have died with Christ (Col. 3:3), and that we are to "consider ourselves dead" (Rom. 6:11), and "put off the old self" (Eph. 4:22). But none of that means the same human being is not in view throughout life. It means that there was an old nature, an old character, or principle, or bent, that needs to be done away with.

So the way to think about your new heart, new spirit, new nature is that it is still you and so needs to be forgiven and cleansed—that's the point of the reference to water. My guilt must be washed away. Cleansing with water is a picture of that. Jeremiah 33:8 puts it like this: "I will cleanse them from all the guilt of their sin against me, and I will forgive all the guilt of their sin and rebellion against me." So the person that we are—that continues to exist—must be forgiven, and the guilt washed away.

THE NEED TO BE NEW

But forgiveness and cleansing are not enough. I need to be new. I need to be transformed. I need life. I need a new way of seeing and thinking and valuing. That's why Ezekiel speaks of a new heart and a new spirit in verses 26–27: "I will give you a new heart, and a new spirit I will put within you. And I will remove the heart of stone from your flesh and give you a heart of flesh. And I will put my *Spirit* within you, and cause you to walk in my statutes and be careful to obey my rules."

Here's the way I understand those verses: To be sure, the heart of stone means the dead heart that was unfeeling and unresponsive to spiritual reality—the heart you had before the new birth. It could respond with passion and desire to lots of things. But it was a stone toward the spiritual truth and beauty of Jesus Christ and the glory of God and the path of holiness. That is what has to change if we are to see the kingdom of God.

So in the new birth, God takes out the heart of stone and puts in a heart of flesh. The word flesh doesn't mean "merely human" as it does in John 3:6 ("that which is born of the flesh is flesh").

It means soft and living and responsive and feeling, instead of being a lifeless stone. In the new birth, our dead, stony boredom with Christ is replaced by a heart that senses the worth of Jesus.

Then when Ezekiel says in verses 26–27, "A new spirit I will put within you....And I will put my Spirit within you, and cause you to walk in my statutes," I think he means that in the new birth, God puts a living, supernatural, spiritual life in our heart, and that new life—that new spirit—is the working of the Holy Spirit himself giving shape and character to our new heart.

The picture I have in my mind is that this new warm, touchable, responsive, living heart is like a soft lump of clay, and the Holy Spirit presses himself up into it and gives spiritual, moral shape to it according to his own shape. By being himself within us, our heart and mind take on his character—his spirit (cf. Eph. 4:23).

Receive Him As Your Treasure

So now let's step back and sum up these last two chapters. What happens in the new birth? In the new birth, the Holy Spirit supernaturally gives us new spiritual life by connecting us with Jesus Christ through faith. Or, to say it another way, the Spirit unites us to Christ where there is cleansing for our sins (pictured by water), and he replaces our hard, unresponsive heart with a soft heart that treasures Jesus above all things and is being transformed by the presence of the Spirit into the kind of heart that loves to do the will of God (Ezek. 36:27).

We will have much more to say about the role of faith in the new birth and how a person may seek the new birth and may help others seek it. But you need not wait. If your heart is drawn to the truth and beauty of Christ, receive him as your life. John holds out this amazing promise: "To all who did receive him, who believed in his name, he gave the right to become children of God" (John 1:12).

PART TWO

WHY MUST WE BE BORN AGAIN?

And you were dead in the trespasses and sins in which you once walked, following the course of this world, following the prince of the power of the air, the spirit that is now at work in the sons of disobedience—among whom we all once lived in the passions of our flesh, carrying out the desires of the body and the mind, and were by nature children of wrath, like the rest of mankind. But God, being rich in mercy, because of the great love with which he loved us, even when we were dead in our trespasses, made us alive together with Christ—by grace you have been saved—and raised us up with him and seated us with him in the heavenly places in Christ Jesus, so that in the coming ages he might show the immeasurable riches of his grace in kindness toward us in Christ Jesus. For by grace you have been saved through faith. And this is not your own doing; it is the gift of God, not a result of works, so that no one may boast. For we are his workmanship, created in Christ Jesus for good works, which God prepared beforehand, that we should walk in them.

Ephesians 2:1–10

3

We Are Spiritually Dead

One of the greatest books about God ever written, John Calvin's *Institutes of the Christian Religion*, begins with this sentence: "Nearly all the wisdom we possess, that is to say, true and sound wisdom, consists of two parts: the knowledge of God and of ourselves."[11] What we may need reminding of in our day is not that the knowledge of God is difficult to comprehend and to embrace—that's more or less obvious—but that the knowledge of *ourselves* is just as difficult to comprehend and to embrace. Indeed, it may be more difficult, first, because a true knowledge of ourselves assumes a true knowledge of God, and second, because we tend to think we *do* know ourselves, when in fact, the depths of our condition are beyond our comprehension without the help of God.

11 Calvin, *Institutes of the Christian Religion*, 35, (I, 1, 1).

Who Can Know the Human Heart?

The prophet Jeremiah wrote, "The heart is deceitful above all things, and desperately sick; who can understand it?" (Jer. 17:9). David said in Psalm 19:12, "Who can discern his errors? Declare me innocent from hidden faults." In other words, we never get to the bottom of our sinfulness. If our forgiveness depended on the fullness of the knowledge of our sins, we would all perish. No one knows the extent of his sinfulness. It is deeper than anyone can fathom.

But the Bible does not leave us without help to know ourselves. The fact that we cannot know fully how sinful we are, does not mean we cannot know our sinfulness deeply and truly. The Bible has a clear and devastating message about the state of our souls. And the reason it does is so that we will know what we need and shout for joy when God gives it to us.

We have heard Jesus say in John 3:7, "You must be born again." And in John 3:3, "Unless one is born again he cannot see the kingdom of God." In other words, being born again is infinitely serious. Heaven and hell are hanging in the balance. We will not see the kingdom of God unless we are born again. So, having dealt with the question *What?* we now turn to the question *Why?*

Why is the new birth so necessary? Why isn't some other remedy sufficient, like turning over a new leaf, or moral improvement, or self-discipine? Why do we need this radical, spiritual, supernatural thing called new birth or regeneration? That's the question addressed in Chapters 3–5.

Diagnosis: Dead; Remedy: Life

The text where we take our beginning is Ephesians 2. Two times, in verses 1 and 5, Paul says that we are dead in our trespasses. Verse 1: "*You were dead* in the trespasses and sins..." Verses 4–5: "But God, being rich in mercy, because of the great love with which he loved us, even *when we were dead* in our trespasses, made us alive together with Christ—by grace you have been saved." So two times Paul describes us as "dead."

And the remedy for this in verse 5 is: "God made us alive." We will never experience the fullness of the greatness of God's love for us if we don't see his love in relation to our former deadness, because verse 4 says that the greatness of his love is shown precisely in this: that it makes us alive when we were dead. "But God, being rich in mercy, because of the great love with which he loved us, even when we were dead in our trespasses, made us alive together with Christ." Because of his great love for us, he made us alive. If we don't know that we were dead, we will not know the fullness of the love of God.

I take this miracle ("he made us alive") to be virtually the same as what Jesus calls the new birth. Once we had no spiritual life, and then God raised us from that state of spiritual deadness. And now we are alive. This is the same as Jesus' saying that we must be "born of the Spirit" (John 3:5) and "It is the Spirit who gives life" (John 6:63).

NEW COVENANT LOVE

So we can say then that the work of regeneration, the work of new birth, the work of being made alive, flows from the richness of God's mercy and the greatness of his love. "But God, (1) *being rich in mercy*, (2) *because of the great love with which he loved us*, even when we were dead in our trespasses, made us alive together with Christ." This is New Covenant love (as we saw in Chapter 2). This is the kind of love God has for his bride.

He finds her dead (Ezek. 16:4–8),[12] and he gives his Son to die for her, and then he makes her alive. And he keeps her forever. "I give them eternal life," Jesus said, "and they will never perish, and no one will snatch them out of my hand" (John 10:28).

So the question is: What does this mean? This deadness? There are at least ten answers in the New Testament. If we consider them honestly and prayerfully, they will humble us very deeply and cause us to be amazed at the gift of the new birth. So what I aim to do is to talk about seven of them in this chapter and three of them in the next chapter along with the larger question: *Do we really need to be changed?* Can't we just be forgiven and justified? Wouldn't that get us to heaven?

Here are seven of the biblical explanations of our condition apart from the new birth and why it is so necessary.

1. *Apart from the new birth, we are dead in trespasses and sins (Eph. 2:1–2).*

Dead implies lifeless. Not physically or morally lifeless, but spiritually lifeless. Verse 1: We are "walking" and "following" the world. Verse 2: We have "passions" of the flesh, and we carry out the "desires of the body and the mind." So we are not dead in the sense that we can't sin. We are dead in the sense that we

---

12 "On the day you were born your cord was not cut, nor were you washed with water to cleanse you, nor rubbed with salt, nor wrapped in swaddling cloths. No eye pitied you, to do any of these things to you out of compassion for you, but you were cast out on the open field, for you were abhorred, on the day that you were born. And when I passed by you and saw you wallowing in your blood, I said to you in your blood, 'Live!' I made you flourish like a plant of the field. And you grew up and became tall and arrived at full adornment. Your breasts were formed, and your hair had grown; yet you were naked and bare. When I passed by you again and saw you, behold, you were at the age for love, and I spread the corner of my garment over you and covered your nakedness; I made my vow to you and entered into a covenant with you, declares the Lord GOD, and you became mine" (Ezek. 16:4–8).

cannot see or savor the glory of Christ. We are spiritually dead. We are unresponsive to God and Christ and this word. Consider now how this is unfolded in nine other descriptions of our condition before new birth happens (six of them in this chapter and three in the next).

2. Apart from the new birth, we are by nature children of wrath (Eph. 2:3).

Verse 3: "We were by nature *children of wrath*, like the rest of mankind." The point of saying this is to make clear that our problem is not just in what we *do* but in what we *are*. Apart from new birth, I *am* my problem. You are not my main problem. My parents were not my main problem. My enemies are not my main problem. *I* am my main problem. Not my deeds, and not my circumstances, and not the people in my life, but *my nature* is my deepest personal problem.

I did not first have a good nature and then do bad things and get a bad nature. "Behold, I was brought forth in iniquity, and in sin did my mother conceive me" (Ps. 51:5). This is who I am. My nature is selfish and self-centered and demanding and very skilled in making you feel like the problem. And if your first response to that statement is *I know people like that*, you may be totally blind to the deceitfulness of your own heart. Our first response should not be finger-pointing. That's part of the problem. Our first response should be contrition.

Paul describes our nature before the new birth as "children of wrath." In other words, the wrath of God belongs to us the way a parent belongs to a child. Our nature is so rebellious and so selfish and so callous toward the majesty of God that his holy anger is a natural and right response to us.

3. *Apart from the new birth, we love darkness and hate the light*
(John 3:19–20).

John 3:19–20:

> This is the judgment: the light has come into the world,
> and people loved the darkness rather than the light because
> their works were evil. For everyone who does wicked
> things hates the light and does not come to the light, lest
> his works should be exposed.

This word from Jesus spells out some of what our nature is like
apart from the new birth. We are not neutral when spiritual
light approaches. We resist it. And we are not neutral when
spiritual darkness envelops us. We embrace it. Love and hate
are active in the unregenerate heart. And they move in exactly
the wrong directions—hating what should be loved and loving
what should be hated.

4. *Apart from the new birth, our hearts are hard like stone*
(Ezek. 36:26; Eph. 4:18).

We saw this in the previous chapter from Ezekiel 36:26 where
God says, "I will remove the heart of stone from your flesh and
give you a heart of flesh." Here in Ephesians 4:18, Paul traces our
condition back through darkness to alienation, to ignorance, to
hardness of heart. "They are darkened in their understanding,
alienated from the life of God because of the ignorance that is in
them, due to their hardness of heart."

At the bottom of our problem is not ignorance. There is something
deeper: "…the ignorance that is in them, due to their hardness of
heart." Our ignorance is guilty ignorance, not innocent ignorance.
It is rooted in hard and resistant hearts. Paul says in Romans 1:18
that we suppress the truth in unrighteousness. Ignorance is not our
biggest problem. Hardness and resistance are.

5. Apart from the new birth, we are unable to submit to God or please God (Rom. 8:7–8).

In Romans 8:7, Paul says, "The mind that is set on the flesh [literally: the mind of the flesh] is hostile to God, for it does not submit to God's law; indeed, *it cannot.* Those who are in the flesh *cannot* please God." We can tell from the next verse what Paul means by "the mind of the flesh" and being "in the flesh." He says in verse 9, "You, however, are not in the flesh but in the Spirit, if in fact the Spirit of God dwells in you." In other words, he is contrasting those who are born again and have the Spirit and those who are not born again and therefore do not have the Spirit but only have the flesh. That which is born of the Spirit is spirit and that which is born of the flesh is flesh (John 3:5).

His point is that without the Holy Spirit, our minds are so resistant to God's authority that we will not, and therefore cannot, submit to him. "The mind of the flesh is hostile to God, for it does not submit to God's law; indeed it cannot." And if we cannot submit to him, we cannot please him. "Those who are in the flesh cannot please God." That is how dead and dark and hard we are toward God until God causes us to be born again.

6. Apart from the new birth, we are unable to accept the gospel (Eph. 4:18; 1 Cor. 2:14).

In 1 Corinthians 2:14, Paul gives us another glimpse into what this deadness and hardness implies for what we are unable to do. He says, "The natural person [that is, the unregenerate person by nature] does not accept the things of the Spirit of God, for they are folly to him, and *he is not able to understand* them because they are spiritually discerned." The problem is not that the things of God are over his head intellectually. The problem is that he sees them as foolish. "He does not accept the things of the Spirit of God, *for* they are folly to him." In fact, they are so foolish to him that he *cannot* grasp them.

Take notice that this is a moral "cannot," not a physical "cannot." When Paul says, "The natural person…is not able to understand them," he means that the heart is so resistant to receiving them that the mind justifies the rebellion of the heart by seeing them as foolish. This rebellion is so complete that the heart really cannot receive the things of the Spirit. This is real inability. But it is not a coerced inability. The unregenerate person cannot because he will not. His preferences for sin are so strong that he cannot choose good. It is a real and terrible bondage. But it is not an innocent bondage.

7. Apart from the new birth, we are unable to come to Christ or embrace him as Lord (John 6:44, 65; 1 Cor. 12:3).

In 1 Corinthians 12:3, Paul declares, "No one can say 'Jesus is Lord' except in the Holy Spirit." He doesn't mean that an actor on a stage, or a hypocrite in a church, cannot say the words "Jesus is Lord" without the Holy Spirit. He means that no one can say it and mean it without being born of the Spirit. It is morally impossible for the dead, dark, hard, resistant heart to celebrate the Lordship of Jesus over his life without being born again.

Or, as Jesus says three times in John 6, no one can come to him unless the Father draws him. And when that drawing brings a person into living connection with Jesus, we call it the new birth. Verse 37: "All that the Father gives me will come to me." Verse 44: "No one can come to me unless the Father who sent me draws him." Verse 65: "No one can come to me unless it is granted him by the Father." All of these wonderful works of drawing, granting, and giving are the work of God in regeneration. Without them we do not come to Christ, because we don't prefer to come. We so strongly prefer self-reliance that we cannot come. That is what has to be changed in the new birth. A new preference, a new ability, is given.

TWO KINDS OF RESPONSE

We end this chapter by going back to the amazingly hope-filled words of Ephesians 2:4–5: "But God, being rich in mercy, because of the great love with which he loved us, even when we were dead in our trespasses, made us alive together with Christ— by grace you have been saved."

There are two ways to respond to this: One is theoretical and impersonal; the other is personal and urgent. One stands back and says: How can this be, and how can that be? The other says: God led me to this chapter today. God spoke in these texts to me today. God's mercy and love and grace seem desperately needed and beautiful to me today. O God, today, I submit to your amazing grace that has brought me here and awakened me and softened me and opened me. Thanks be to God for the riches of his mercy and the greatness of his love and the power of his grace.

That which was from the beginning, which we have heard, which we have seen with our eyes, which we looked upon and have touched with our hands, concerning the word of life—the life was made manifest, and we have seen it, and testify to it and proclaim to you the eternal life, which was with the Father and was made manifest to us—that which we have seen and heard we proclaim also to you, so that you too may have fellowship with us; and indeed our fellowship is with the Father and with his Son Jesus Christ. And we are writing these things so that our joy may be complete. This is the message we have heard from him and proclaim to you, that God is light, and in him is no darkness at all. If we say we have fellowship with him while we walk in darkness, we lie and do not practice the truth. But if we walk in the light, as he is in the light, we have fellowship with one another, and the blood of Jesus his Son cleanses us from all sin. If we say we have no sin, we deceive ourselves, and the truth is not in us. If we confess our sins, he is faithful and just to forgive us our sins and to cleanse us from all unrighteousness. If we say we have not sinned, we make him a liar, and his word is not in us.

1 John 1:1–10

4

WE ARE WILLING SLAVES
TO SIN AND SATAN

In the previous chapter, we launched our answer to the question
Why must we be born again? We started with Ephesians 2:4–5:
"But God, being rich in mercy, because of the great love with
which he loved us, even when we were dead in our trespasses,
made us alive together with Christ—by grace you have been
saved." I said that "God made us alive" is virtually the same
as the new birth. The reason Paul gives for why we need this
miracle is that we were dead. "Even when *we were dead* in our
trespasses, God made us alive."

This is what we need—the miracle of spiritual life created in
our hearts. And the reason we need it is that we are spiritually
dead. We are unable to see or savor the beauty and worth of
Christ for who he really is. Those who are not born again
do not say with Paul, "I count everything as loss because
of the surpassing worth of knowing Christ Jesus my Lord"
(Phil. 3:8).

Then we began to unpack the meaning of this deadness. I said I would mention ten ways of describing this condition from the New Testament. We have already looked at seven of them:

1 We are dead in trespasses and sins (Eph. 2:1–2).
2 We are by nature children of wrath (Eph. 2:3).
3 We love darkness and hate the light (John 3:19–20).
4 Our hearts are hard like stone (Ezek. 36:26; Eph. 4:18).
5 We are unable to submit to God or please God (Rom. 8:7–8).
6 We are unable to accept the gospel (Eph. 4:18; 1 Cor. 2:14).
7 We are unable to come to Christ or embrace him as Lord (John 6:44, 65; 1 Cor. 12:3).

Now we turn to the last three descriptions of our condition apart from the new birth. The aim in this list is to give us an accurate diagnosis of our disease so that when God applies the remedy at great cost to himself, we will leap for joy and give him some measure of the glory he deserves. We will not sing with authentic amazement the words "Amazing grace, how sweet the sound that saved a wretch like me," unless we know the nature of our "wretchedness." John Newton knew his heart. That's why he wrote the song.

8. Apart from the new birth, we are slaves to sin (Rom. 6:17).

Paul celebrates our liberation from slavery to sin by thanking *God* for it. He says in Romans 6:17, "But *thanks be to God*, that you who were once *slaves of sin* have become obedient from the heart to the standard of teaching to which you were committed." We were once so in love with sin that we could not leave it or kill it.

Then something happened. The new birth happened. God caused us to get a new spiritual life, a new nature that hates sin and loves righteousness. And so Paul thanks God, not man, for this great liberation: "Thanks be to God, that you who were once slaves of sin have become obedient from the heart." Until God awakens us from spiritual death and gives us the life that finds joy in killing sin and being holy, we are slaves and cannot get free. That's why the new birth is necessary.

9. Apart from the new birth, we are slaves of Satan (Eph. 2:1–2; 2 Tim. 2:24–26).

This is one of the terrible things about spiritual deadness. Our deadness is not unresponsive to the devil. It is perfectly in tune with the devil. Look at the way Paul describes our deadness in Ephesians 2:1–2: "You were dead in the trespasses and sins in which you once walked, following the course of this world, *following the prince of the power of the air*, the spirit that is now at work in the sons of disobedience." In other words, the mark of unregenerate persons is that their desires and choices "accord with" the prince of the power of the air. The unregenerate may scoff at the very idea of a devil. And of course, nothing is more in line with the father of lies than the denial that he exists.

But the bondage to the devil is most clearly mentioned in 2 Timothy 2:24–26. This is an exhortation to ministers about how to liberate people from the bondage of the devil:

> The Lord's servant must not be quarrelsome but kind to everyone, able to teach, patiently enduring evil, correcting his opponents with gentleness. God may perhaps grant them repentance leading to a knowledge of the truth, and they may come to their senses and escape from the snare of the devil, after being captured by him to do his will.

When Paul says that "God may perhaps grant them repentance leading to a knowledge of the truth," that is virtually what happens in the new birth. And here is the key to liberating people from the captivity of the devil. God grants repentance— that is, he awakens the life that sees the ugliness and danger of sin and the beauty and worth of Christ. That truth sets the prisoner free.

It's what happens when a person in the dark fondles an ebony brooch hanging around his neck, and then the lights go on and he sees it's not a brooch but a cockroach, and flings it away. That's how people are set free from the devil. And until God does that miracle of new birth, we stay in bondage to the father of lies because we love to be able to tell ourselves whatever we please. We keep fondling smooth roaches and warm fuzzy tarantulas in the dark.

10. Apart from the new birth, no good thing dwells in us (Rom. 7:18).

Now this is a statement that is unintelligible to the unregenerate who know very well that they do many good things and that they could do much more evil than they do. The statement makes no sense—that there is no good in us before new birth—without the conviction that everything good that God has made and that God sustains is ruined when it is not done in reliance on God's grace and in pursuit of God's glory.

So, of course, in one sense the human person (the soul, the mind, the heart, the brain, the eye, the hand) and human social structures (marriage, family, government, business) are all good. God made them, ordains them, sustains them. It is right that they exist. But they all exist for the glory of God. God commands that we love him with all our heart and soul and mind (Matt. 22:37). He commands that we use all that he has made by relying on his grace and in order to show his worth (1 Pet. 4:11). Where people use all that God has made without relying on his grace and without aiming to show his worth, they prostitute God's creation. They make it the instrument of unbelief. And they ruin it.

So when Paul says in Romans 7:18, "I know that nothing good dwells in me, that is, in my flesh," this is the reason he adds the qualifier "that is, in my flesh." There is something good in Paul after the new birth. Faith is good. The Holy Spirit is good. The new spiritual nature is good. Growing holiness is good. But in his flesh, that is, in the person he is by nature apart from the new birth, there is no good thing. All that was created good is ruined by being made the servant of man-centered concerns, not God-centered concerns.

This is our tenfold condition apart from the new birth. Apart from regeneration we are, to use the words of Paul in Ephesians 2:12, "separated from Christ, alienated from the commonwealth of Israel and strangers to the covenants of promise, having no hope and without God in the world." This is why we must be born again. Without the new birth, our condition is hopeless, and we cannot fix it with moral improvement. Dead men do not do better. Dead men need one thing before anything else can happen: They must be made alive. They must be born again.

THE OTHER HALF OF THE QUESTION

Until now I have been asking only half of the *why* question. The question really has two meanings. The one we've been answering is: Why don't I have spiritual life and why can't I get it on my own? Our answer has been that we are rebellious and selfish and demanding and hard and resistant to spiritual things and unable to see the beauty and worth of Christ and therefore unable to come to him for life. And that's why we need a supernatural work of God to make us alive. We need to be born again. That's the first way to ask the question *Why is the new birth necessary?*

But there is another way. The question also means: What do you need the new birth for? What does it bring about that you need in the future? What can't you have without it? The first way of asking the question looks back and asks what our condition is that makes the new birth necessary. And the second way of asking the question looks forward and asks what must happen for our future joy that only the new birth can bring about? That's what we turn to now.

WHAT WON'T WE HAVE WITHOUT THE NEW BIRTH?

I'll try to answer this new question in summary form in the rest of this chapter, and then work it out in practical detail in the following chapter. What won't we have without the new birth?

Jesus' answer was simple and sweeping and devastating: "Truly, truly, I say to you, unless one is born again he cannot see the kingdom of God" (John 3:3). Without the new birth, we will not see the kingdom of God. That is, we will not go to heaven. We will perish eternally. What won't we have without the new birth? We won't have anything good. We will have only suffering forever.

But it's important that we show why this is so. We need to unpack the way God saves us through the new birth—the way he gets us to the kingdom. We need to see the connection between the new birth and what God has done to save us through the death and resurrection of Jesus.

So I will give five interrelated answers to the question, first in a negative form, and then finally, in a positive form. What won't we have without the new birth? First, negatively:

1 Without the new birth, we won't have saving faith, but only unbelief (John 1:11–13; 1 John 5:1; Eph. 2:8–9; Phil. 1:29; 1 Tim. 1:14; 2 Tim. 1:3).

2 Without the new birth, we won't have justification, but only condemnation (Rom. 8:1; 2 Cor. 5:21; Gal. 2:17; Phil. 3:9).

3 Without the new birth, we won't be the children of God, but the children of the devil (1 John 3:9–10).

4 Without the new birth, we won't bear the fruit of love by the Holy Spirit but only the fruit of death (Rom. 6:20–21; 7:4–6; 15:16; 1 Cor. 1:2; 2 Cor. 5:17; Eph. 2:10; Gal. 5:6; 2 Thess. 2:13; 1 Pet. 1:2; 1 John 3:14).

5 Without the new birth, we won't have eternal joy in fellowship with God, but only eternal misery with the devil and his angels (Matt. 25:41; John 3:3; Rom. 6:23; Rev. 2:11; 20:15).

To know ourselves and to know the greatness of Christ and of our salvation, we need to know how the new birth relates to those five destinies. We will see more of this relationship in the next chapter. But I conclude here by saying them again, only this time positively and in the words of Scripture. Notice especially how each builds on the ones before.

1 When God causes us to be born again, saving *faith* is awakened, and we are united to Christ. 1 John 5:1: "Everyone who *believes* that Jesus is the Christ *has been born* of God." Not *will be* born of God, but *has been* born of God. Our first faith is the flicker of life through the new birth.

2 When the new birth awakens faith, and unites us to Christ, we are *justified*—that is, counted righteous—through that faith. Romans 5:1: "Since we have been justified by faith, we have peace with God through our Lord Jesus Christ." New birth awakens faith, and faith looks to Christ for righteousness, and God credits righteousness to us on the basis of Christ alone through faith alone.

3 When new birth awakens faith and unites us to Christ, all the legal obstacles to our acceptance with God are removed

through justification. So God adopts us into his family and conforms us to the image of his Son. John 1:12: "To all who did receive him, who believed in his name, he gave the right to become children of God, who were born, not of blood nor of the will of the flesh nor of the will of man, but of God." We are born again from God, not from the will of man, and we believe on Christ and receive him, and God makes us his *legal heirs and spiritual children*.

4 When the new birth wakens faith and we are united to Christ, and all condemnation is replaced with justification and the Spirit of adoption moves into our lives, he produces *the fruit of love*. Galatians 5:6: "In Christ Jesus neither circumcision nor uncircumcision counts for anything, but only faith working through love." 1 John 3:14: "We know that we have passed out of death into life, because we love the brothers." Where there is new birth, there is love.

5 Finally, when the new birth wakens faith and unites us to Christ, who is our righteousness, and unleashes the sanctifying power of the Holy Spirit, we are on the narrow way that leads to heaven. And the pinnacle of heaven's joys will be eternal *fellowship with God*. "This is eternal life, that they know you the only true God, and Jesus Christ whom you have sent" (John 17:3). The pinnacle of the joy of our new life is God himself.

This is what we will miss if we are not born again. The reason for being born again is not only that we are dead without it, but that we miss everything good forever without it. This is why Jesus said, "You must be born again" (John 3:3, 7).

That which was from the beginning, which we have heard, which we have seen with our eyes, which we looked upon and have touched with our hands, concerning the word of life—the life was made manifest, and we have seen it, and testify to it and proclaim to you the eternal life, which was with the Father and was made manifest to us—that which we have seen and heard we proclaim also to you, so that you too may have fellowship with us; and indeed our fellowship is with the Father and with his Son Jesus Christ. And we are writing these things so that our joy may be complete. This is the message we have heard from him and proclaim to you, that God is light, and in him is no darkness at all. If we say we have fellowship with him while we walk in darkness, we lie and do not practice the truth. But if we walk in the light, as he is in the light, we have fellowship with one another, and the blood of Jesus his Son cleanses us from all sin. If we say we have no sin, we deceive ourselves, and the truth is not in us. If we confess our sins, he is faithful and just to forgive us our sins and to cleanse us from all unrighteousness. If we say we have not sinned, we make him a liar, and his word is not in us.

1 John 1:1–10

5

FAITH, JUSTIFICATION, ADOPTION, PURIFICATION, GLORIFICATION

This chapter was first composed at Christmastime. Therefore, it attempts to do two things at once. It makes the connection between the incarnation of Christ and regeneration—that's the Christmas part—and it attempts to carry forward the question in the previous chapter: *What will we miss out on if we are not born again?* If you read the chapter with those two questions in mind, you may find your way more easily.

WHY CHRISTMAS?

Twice in 1 John 3:1–10 we are told why Christmas happened—that is, why the eternal, divine Son of God came into the world as a human being. In verse 5, John says, "You know that he appeared to take away sins, and in him there is no sin." So the sinlessness of Christ is affirmed—"in him there is no sin." And the reason for his coming is affirmed—"he appeared to take away sins."

Then, in the second part of verse 8, John says, "The reason the Son of God appeared was to destroy the works of the devil."

And the specific focus John has in mind when he says "works of the devil" is the sin that the devil promotes. We see this in the first part of verse 8: "Whoever makes a practice of sinning is of the devil, for the devil has been sinning from the beginning." So the works of the devil that Jesus came to destroy are the works of sin.

Two times John tells us that Christmas happened—the Son of God became human—to take away sin, that is, to destroy the works of the devil, namely, sin. So Jesus was born of a virgin by the Holy Spirit (Matt. 1:18, 20), and "increased in wisdom and in stature and in favor with God and man" (Luke 2:52), and was perfectly obedient and sinless in all his life and ministry, all the way to the point of death, even death on a cross (Phil. 2:5–8; Heb. 4:15)—in order to destroy the works of the devil—to take away sin.

JESUS' INCARNATION AND OUR REGENERATION

One of the questions we are asking in this chapter is: *What is the connection between Jesus' birth and our new birth?* What is the relationship between Jesus' incarnation and our regeneration? To answer this question, let's build a bridge from the previous chapter to this text here in 1 John 3:1–10.

In the last chapter, we saw that when we ask why we need to be born again, the answer could look backward to our miserable condition in sin, or could look forward to the great things we will miss if we are not born again—like entering the kingdom of God. We gave ten answers for why we need to be born again in the first sense—looking back on what we were apart from new birth. And we gave five answers for why we need to be born again in the second sense—looking forward to what we will not enjoy if we aren't born again.

THE GREAT LOVE OF GOD

Now the bridge between that chapter and this text in 1 John 3 is *the great love of God* that gives life to people who are at enmity with God and are dead in trespasses and sins. Ephesians 2:4–5 puts it like this: "But God, being rich in mercy, because of *the great love* with which he loved us, even when we were dead in our trespasses, made us alive together with Christ." So the greatness of the love of God is magnified in that it gives spiritual life—that is new birth—to those who have no claim on God at all. We were spiritually dead, and in our deadness we were walking in lockstep with God's archenemy, the devil (Eph. 2:2). The justice of God would have been well served if we had perished forever in that condition. But for that very reason, our new birth—our being made alive—is a magnificent display of the greatness of the love of God. We owe our spiritual life, and all its impulses, to the greatness and the freedom of the love of God.

Now this is the bridge to 1 John 3:1–2, namely, the great love of God for those who are not yet in his family.

> See what kind of love the Father has given to us [there's the link with the greatness of the love of God], that we should be called children of God; and so we are. The reason why the world does not know us is that it did not know him. Beloved [loved ones!], we are God's children now, and what we will be has not yet appeared; but we know that when he appears we shall be like him, because we shall see him as he is.

Consider four observations that connect this text with the greatness of the love of God in Ephesians 2:4, and with our question in the previous chapter about why we need to be born again.

1. Made God's Children

First, when verse 1 says that we are "called" the children of God, it doesn't mean we were already the children of God but not called that, and then God called us that. No, it means that we were *not* children of God. We were like the rest of the world referred to in verse 1. We were dead and outside the family. Then God called us children. And we became children of God. Notice the words "and so we are." Verse 1: We are "called children of God; and so we are." The point is: God *made* us his children. He did it with his sovereign call—the way he raised Lazarus from the dead. He simply called him. And the call imparted life (John 11:43). This is the new birth. God made us alive just as he did in Ephesians 2:5.

2. The Greatness of the Love of God

Second, this new birth into the family of God is owing to the greatness of the love of God here in 1 John 3, just like it was in Ephesians 2:4–5. "See [Look! This is amazing!] what kind of *love* the Father has given us that we should be called the children of God." John was amazed, just as Paul was—just as we should be—that rebels, enemies, and dead, unresponsive slaves to sin like us are made alive, born again, and called the children of God. John wanted us to feel the wonder of it. That's why he begins with "See!"

3. Our Final Perfection Secured

Third, this amazing love of God that gave us life when we were dead, and caused us to be born again, and brought us into the family of God, secures our final perfection in the presence of God forever. Notice the way verse 2 connects three things: the love of God for us, our present life as his children, and the future we long for. "Beloved, we are God's children now, and what we will be has not yet appeared; but we know that when he appears we shall be like him, because we shall see him as he is."

John sees an unbreakable link between what we are now and what we will be when Christ comes. He expresses it with the words "we know." "We are God's children now, and what we will be has not yet appeared [our perfect conformity to Christ awaits his coming]; but we know that when he appears we shall be like him."

In other words, the perfection of our sonship is surely coming. We know it is. How? Because of his love, we are his children now. And all that's left in our adoption is the consummation of our transformation when we see Jesus face to face. His presence will complete it for all the children of God. And "we are God's children now."

4. The Necessity of the New Birth

Now we see how John is beginning to address the question from the last chapter: What will we miss if we are not born again? So our fourth observation is simply to make explicit something obvious in what we've said so far: The new birth is a necessary prerequisite and a guarantee of our future perfection in the presence of Christ forever. Or, to put it the way Jesus did: "Truly, truly, I say to you, unless one is born again he cannot see the kingdom of God." But if you *are* born again, you *will* see the kingdom of God. Or to use the words of 1 John 3, you *will* see Christ face to face and be perfected and spend eternity with joy in his presence.

So here we are with John's answer to the question *Why must we be born again?* John's answer is: Because if you are not born again, you will not look upon Jesus someday and in the twinkling of an eye be changed into his image. Instead, you will remain under the wrath of God (as Jesus says in John 3:36). Or, to put it positively, if the immeasurable love of God causes you to be born again and gives you new spiritual life in union with Jesus, you know that when he appears you will be like him. Because of the new birth, you know you will enter the kingdom of God. That's why we must be born again.

JESUS' BIRTH AND OUR NEW BIRTH

Now we are also in a position to answer the other question this Christmas-oriented chapter is posing: What is the connection between *Jesus'* birth and *our* new birth? What is the relationship between Jesus' *incarnation* and our *regeneration*? Could not God have simply caused sinners to be born again and then finally conformed them to his own character in heaven, without sending his Son into the world? Did there need to be an incarnation of the Son of God and a perfect life of obedience and a death on the cross?

The answer is: The new birth and all of its effects, including faith and justification and purification and final conformity to Christ in heaven, would not be possible without the incarnation and life and death of Jesus—without Christmas and Good Friday and Easter.

We get a glimpse of this here in John's First Epistle.

BORN AGAIN TO BEHOLD AND BELIEVE THE GOD-MAN

First, consider that the aim of the new birth is to enable us to believe specifically in the *incarnate* Jesus Christ. If there were no incarnate Jesus Christ to believe in, then the new birth would not happen. Look at 1 John 5:1: "Everyone who believes that Jesus is the Christ [that is everyone who believes that this incarnate Jewish man from Nazareth is the promised divine Messiah] has been born of God." That means that the Holy Spirit causes people to be born again with a view to creating faith in the incarnate God-man, Jesus Christ (see 1 John 4:2–3). That's the aim of the new birth. And so faith in Jesus Christ is the first evidence that the new birth has happened. "Everyone who believes that Jesus is the Christ has been born of God." Faith is the sign that the new birth has happened.

NEW LIFE THROUGH UNION WITH THE INCARNATE ONE

But that's not the only reason the incarnation is necessary for the new birth. The incarnation of the Son of God is also necessary because the life we have through the new birth is *life in union with the incarnate Christ*. Jesus said, "I am the living bread that came down from heaven. If anyone eats of this bread, he will live forever. And the bread that I will give for the life of the world is my flesh" (John 6:51). That life that we have in union with Christ is the life that Jesus obtained for us by the life he lived and the death he died in the flesh.

Consider 1 John 5:10–12, and keep in mind as you read that the Son of God here is the incarnate Son of God. "Whoever believes in the Son of God has the testimony in himself....And this is the testimony, that God gave us eternal life, and this life is in his Son. Whoever has the Son has life; whoever does not have the Son of God does not have life."

In other words, the new birth gives us life by bringing us into spiritual connection with Jesus Christ. He is our life. His new life in us, with all the changes that it brings, is the testimony of God that we are his children. And this life is the life of the incarnate Son of God. "And the Word became flesh and dwelt among us....And from his fullness [the fullness of the incarnate one] we have all received grace upon grace" (John 1:14–16)—that is new birth, new life.

No Incarnation, No Regeneration

So if there were no incarnation—no Christmas—there would be no regeneration for these two reasons: 1) If there were no incarnation, there would be no incarnate Jesus Christ to behold and believe in, and that's the aim of the new birth. So the new birth would not happen. 2) If there were no incarnation, there would be no vital union or connection between us and the incarnate Christ, and so the new birth would abort because there would be no source of new saving, forgiving life.

Christianity is not a kind of spirituality that floats amorphously through various religions. It is historically rooted in the person of Jesus Christ. Therefore, the Scripture says, "Whoever has the Son has life; whoever does not have the Son of God does not have life" (1 John 5:12). "Whoever does not honor the Son does not honor the Father who sent him" (John 5:23). "The one who rejects me," Jesus said, "rejects him who sent me" (Luke 10:16). If there is no incarnation, there is no union with the Son or with the Father, and no regeneration—and no salvation.

INCARNATION AND PURIFICATION

So without the incarnation of the Son of God as the Messiah, there would be no regeneration and no saving faith. And we may add then briefly, there would be no justification and no purification. And without these, no final glorification. You can see the connections with justification and purification in 1 John 3:3–5:

> Everyone who thus hopes in him [in other words, every child of God who is assured of being made like Christ when he comes] purifies himself as he is pure. Everyone who makes a practice of sinning also practices lawlessness; sin is lawlessness. You know that he appeared to take away sins, and in him there is no sin.

Both justification and purification are implied here. Purification is explicit. John says: If you have experienced the new birth, you will love the day of Christ's appearing and long for the day when you will be transformed into his perfect likeness (as verse 2 says, "when he appears we shall be like him"). And then, he says in verse 3, "Everyone who thus hopes in him *purifies* himself as he is pure." That means everyone who loves the day of his final purification loves purity now, and hates impurity now, and fights sin now.

Which means that the new birth, which awakens faith and fills us with love for that last great day of purification, produces the fight for purity. And so, since there is no regeneration without the incarnation, there will be no purification now, and no final Christ-like purity in the end, if there is no incarnation.

Christianity is not the general program for moral transformation that marks most religions. The transformation it calls for is historically rooted in the person of Jesus Christ. The new birth awakens faith in him. And he—the incarnate one—secures our final purification. And we, with that unshakable hope in him, purify ourselves as he is pure.

INCARNATION AND JUSTIFICATION

Which leaves one last great work of Christ to touch on: justification. It is hinted at in 1 John 3:4–5. Right after saying that those who are born again purify themselves as Christ is pure, John says something about sin that seems out of the blue. He says, "Everyone who makes a practice of sinning also practices lawlessness; sin is lawlessness. You know that he appeared to take away sins, and in him there is no sin."

What's the point of telling us suddenly that "sin is lawlessness" and that therefore all sins are lawlessness—and then adding that Christ appeared "to take away sins"? I think the point is this. He wants to make clear to us that the great work of Christ in saving us from sin is not only a work of purification.

The language of cleansing and purifying fail to deal with a huge and terrible dimension of our sin, namely, that all sin is lawbreaking. We don't only incur defilement that has to be purified; we incur guilt that has to be forgiven, and wrath that has to be propitiated, and a falling short of the righteousness that God requires.

That's why he says in verses 4–5, "Sin is lawlessness. You know that he appeared to take away sins." This "take away sins" is not mere cleansing. This is the work of Christ in taking away the guilt of sin, and the wrath of God that sin deserves. And how did Christ do this? He did it by his incarnation and life and death. Here are two texts from 1 John to show how John thought about this.

First, 1 John 4:10: "In this is love, not that we have loved God but that he loved us and sent his Son to be the propitiation for our sins." He sent his Son—that's the incarnation—to die in our place and so absorb the wrath of God that we deserved. That is what propitiation is: It is an act that satisfies the holy wrath of God. Because of Christ crucified, God's punitive wrath is removed forever from those who are born again.

Second, 1 John 2:1: "My little children, I am writing these things to you so that you may not sin. But if anyone does sin, we have an advocate with the Father, Jesus Christ the righteous." Why is Jesus in heaven explicitly called "the righteous" when he is described as the advocate we need because of our sin? It's because what he pleads before the Father is not only his blood, but also his righteousness. Which is why 1 John 3:5 says, "In him there is no sin." The perfection we do not have, Jesus provided. The judgment we do not want, Jesus bore.

Christmas Was Not Optional

All of this unspeakably wonderful news could not have come to pass if the Son of God had never become man. The incarnation was necessary for all this to come true. The Son of God became the God-man. The Word became flesh (John 1:14). If there had been no incarnation, there would have been no regeneration, no faith, no justification, no purification, and no final glorification.

Christmas was not optional. Therefore, God—being rich in mercy, out of the great love with which he loved us, while we were dead in trespasses—sent his Son into the world to live without sin and die in our place. What a great love the Father has shown to us! What a great obedience and sacrifice the Lord Jesus gave for us! What a great awakening the Spirit has worked in us to bring us to faith and everlasting life!

Part Three

How Does
the New Birth Come About?

Therefore, preparing your minds for action, and being sober-minded, set your hope fully on the grace that will be brought to you at the revelation of Jesus Christ. As obedient children, do not be conformed to the passions of your former ignorance, but as he who called you is holy, you also be holy in all your conduct, since it is written, "You shall be holy, for I am holy." And if you call on him as Father who judges impartially according to each one's deeds, conduct yourselves with fear throughout the time of your exile, knowing that you were ransomed from the futile ways inherited from your forefathers, not with perishable things such as silver or gold, but with the precious blood of Christ, like that of a lamb without blemish or spot. He was foreknown before the foundation of the world but was made manifest in the last times for the sake of you who through him are believers in God, who raised him from the dead and gave him glory, so that your faith and hope are in God. Having purified your souls by your obedience to the truth for a sincere brotherly love, love one another earnestly from a pure heart, since you have been born again, not of perishable seed but of imperishable, through the living and abiding word of God; for "All flesh is like grass and all its glory like the flower of grass. The grass withers, and the flower falls, but the word of the Lord remains forever." And this word is the good news that was preached to you.

1 Peter 1:13–25

6

RANSOMED, RAISED, AND CALLED

One of the unsettling things about the new birth, which Jesus says we all must experience in order to see the kingdom of God (John 3:3), is that we don't control it. We don't decide to make it happen any more than a baby decides to make his birth happen— or, more accurately, make his conception happen. Or even more accurately: We don't decide to make it happen any more than dead men decide to give themselves life. The reason we need to be born again is that we are dead in our trespasses and sins. That's why we need the new birth, and that's why we can't make it happen. This is one reason why we speak of the *sovereign* grace of God. Or better: This is one reason why we *love* the sovereign grace of God.

Our condition before the new birth is that we treasure sin and self-exaltation so much that we cannot treasure Christ supremely. In other words, we are so rebellious at the root of our fallen human nature that we can't find it in ourselves to humbly see and savor Jesus Christ above all things. And we are guilty for this. This is real evil in us. We are blameworthy for this spiritual hardness and deadness. Our consciences do not excuse us when we are so resistant to Christ that we can't see him as supremely attractive.

FIRE AND HEAT INSEPARABLE

Something has to happen *to* us. Jesus said we must be born again (John 3:3). The Holy Spirit has to work a miracle in our hearts and give us new spiritual life. We were dead, and we need to be made alive. We need ears that can hear truth as supremely desirable, and we need eyes that see Christ and his way of salvation as supremely beautiful. We need hearts that are soft and receptive to the word of God. In short, we need new life. We need to be born again.

The way this happens, as we have seen so far, is that the Spirit of God supernaturally gives us new spiritual life by connecting us with Jesus Christ through faith. The new spiritual life that we receive in the new birth is not separate from union with Jesus, and it is not separate from faith. When God in the riches of his mercy and the greatness of his love and the sovereignty of his grace chooses to regenerate us, he gives us new life by uniting us to Christ. "God gave us eternal life, and this life is in his Son" (1 John 5:11). Our first experience of this is the faith in Jesus that this life brings. There is no separation of time here. When we are born again, we believe. And when we believe, we know we have been born again. When there is fire, there is heat. When there is new birth, there is faith.

NOW THE QUESTION *HOW?*

We have focused so far on two questions: *What is the new birth?* and *Why do we need to be born again?* Now we are turning to the third question: *How are we born again?* or *What is the way we are born again?* Here I am asking the question from God's side and from our side. What is the way God does it? And what is the way we do it? How does God regenerate us? How do we take part in it and how are we involved in it?

You might think I would say that we have no involvement in it, because we are spiritually dead. But the dead are very much involved in their resurrection—after all, they rise! Here is an example of what I mean. When Jesus stood before the grave of Lazarus who had been dead for four days, Lazarus had no part in imparting his new life. He was dead. Jesus, not Lazarus, created the new life.

In John 11:43, Jesus says to the dead Lazarus, "Lazarus, come out." And the next verse says, "The man who had died came out." So Lazarus takes part in this resurrection. He comes out. Christ causes it. Lazarus does it. He is the one who rises from the dead! Christ brings about the resurrection. Lazarus acts out the resurrection. The instant Christ commands Lazarus to rise, Lazarus does the rising. The instant God gives new life, we do the living. The instant the Spirit produces faith, we do the believing.

So that's why I am asking two questions, and not just one question, when I ask *How are we born again?* I am asking: What does God do in our new birth? How are we born again from God's side? And I am asking: What do we do in our new birth? How are we born again from our side? It is the first question that we will be addressing in this chapter. How are we born again from God's side? What is the way God regenerates us?

HOW DOES GOD REGENERATE US?

The answer is given in at least three ways in 1 Peter 1:3–25:

- First, verse 3 says that God caused us to be born again "through the resurrection of Jesus Christ from the dead."
- Second, verse 23 says God caused us to be born again "through the living and abiding word of God." Or, as verse 15 puts it, God called us.

· And third, verse 18 says that God ransomed us from the futile ways inherited from our forefathers.

Imperishability Unites All Three

Before we look at these in more detail, notice first what makes these three events hang together as God's way of causing the new birth. In all three of these works of God, there is a reference to *imperishability*. Verses 3–4:

> Blessed be the God and Father of our Lord Jesus Christ! According to his great mercy, he has caused us to be born again to a living hope through the resurrection of Jesus Christ from the dead, to an inheritance that is imperishable.

So the point is that by the new birth, God means for us to have not just new life but eternal life. Verse 3: We are "born again to a *living hope*." So the emphasis falls on the *hope* of our new life. It lives—and will not die. It inherits an *imperishable* inheritance. That's the emphasis. Our new life in the new birth is forever. We will never die.

Then, notice the same emphasis in verses 18–19:

> ...knowing that you were ransomed from the futile ways inherited from your forefathers, not with perishable things such as silver or gold, but with the precious blood of Christ, like that of a lamb without blemish or spot.

The blood of Christ (v. 19) is the ransom price paid for our life, and this blood is contrasted with the less valuable silver and gold that might have been paid. And the reason silver and gold are less valuable is that they are "perishable." Verse 18: "*not with perishable things* such as silver or gold."

So again the point is that the new life that Jesus ransoms with his blood is not in danger of going back into captivity, because the price he pays for our new life (our new birth) is not perishable.

The blood of Christ is of infinite value, and therefore, its value never runs out. It is an imperishable value. That is how we are ransomed. That's the price of the new life we receive in the new birth. And Jesus paid it for us.

Then, thirdly, notice the same emphasis on imperishability in verse 23: "You have been born again, not of perishable seed but of imperishable, through the living and abiding word of God." Then, Peter quotes Isaiah 40:6–8 in verses 24–25: "For 'All flesh is like grass and all its glory like the flower of grass. The grass withers, and the flower falls, but the word of the Lord remains forever.' And this word is the good news that was preached to you." So the point is the same as with the resurrection in verse 3 and the ransom in verse 18: The seed of God's word is imperishable, and therefore, the life that it generates and sustains is imperishable.

So now we have a summary overview of Peter's emphasis in the new birth. The emphasis is that we are born again to a living hope. In other words, the life God creates in the new birth is eternal life, imperishable life. The new nature that comes into being in the new birth cannot die. It lasts forever. That is what Peter is emphasizing about the new birth. What comes into being in the new birth will never die. I think Peter is emphasizing this because the overarching context of his letter is suffering. Don't be daunted by your suffering. Even if they take your physical life, they cannot take the life you have by the new birth. That is imperishable.

RANSOMED, RAISED, CALLED

Now let's look at these three works of God once more—only this time to see how each of them is a way of bringing about the new birth. Let's take these one at a time and put them in the order that they actually happened: 1) God ransomed us by the blood of Jesus; 2) God raised Jesus from the dead; 3) God called us into life through his living and abiding word.

Verses 18–19: "You were ransomed from the futile ways inherited from your forefathers, not with perishable things such as silver or gold, but with the precious blood of Christ, like that of a lamb without blemish or spot." The point here, in regard to the new birth, is that new eternal life is not possible for enslaved sinners without a ransom being paid. This text implies that we were all in bondage or captivity to ways of thinking and feeling and acting that would have destroyed us. We were under the wrath of God who had handed us over to these futile ways (Rom. 1:21, 24, 26, 28). Slavery to these sinful ways would destroy us if we could not be ransomed from this slavery. God paid this ransom price by sending Christ to bear his own wrath (Rom. 8:3; Gal. 3:13).

This is the rock-solid historical foundation that makes our new birth possible. As a basis for God to unite us to Christ and create faith and give us new life, there had to be some objective, historical events in the life of Jesus Christ, the Son of God. Jesus said in Mark 10:45, "The Son of Man came not to be served but to serve, and to give his life as a ransom for many." This is why the historical event of the incarnation happened.

The Son of Man came "to give his life a ransom for many." This had to happen as the basis of the free and gracious gift of the new birth for undeserving sinners like us. And since the new birth is the gift of eternal life, not just new life, the ransom price had to be imperishable—not like silver or gold. The blood of Christ is infinitely valuable and, therefore, can never lose its ransoming power. The life it obtains lasts forever. So the way God brings about the new birth is by paying a ransom for the eternal life it imparts.

The second objective historical event that had to happen for us to be born again with eternal life was the resurrection of Jesus from the dead. 1 Peter 1:3–4:

> Blessed be the God and Father of our Lord Jesus Christ! According to his great mercy, he has caused us to be born again to a living hope through the resurrection of Jesus

Christ from the dead, to an inheritance that is imperishable, undefiled, and unfading, kept in heaven for you.

"Born again...through the resurrection of Jesus Christ from the dead." So the second way that God brings about the new birth is by raising Jesus from the dead.

The new birth is something that happens in us when the Holy Spirit takes our dead hearts and unites us to Christ by faith so that his life becomes our life. So it makes sense that Jesus must be raised from the dead if we are to have new life in union with him. New birth happens, as we saw in Chapter 5, in union with the incarnate Christ, not simply the eternal Son of God before his incarnation. The new life we get in the new birth is the life of the historical Jesus. Therefore, if he does not rise from the dead, there is no new life to have. So the second way God brings about the new birth is to raise Jesus from the dead.

The third way God causes us to be born again is that he calls us. 1 Peter 1:14–15: "As obedient children, do not be conformed to the passions of your former ignorance, but as he who called you is holy, you also be holy in all your conduct." Peter is telling us to live differently now because of something that happened to us in the past. Verse 15: "As he who called you is holy, you also be holy in all your conduct." This act of calling is the way God causes us to be born again. He ransoms us with the blood of Christ. He raises Christ from the dead. And he calls us to life in union with Christ.

To understand what happened to us when God called us this way, it helps to distinguish it from the general calling that goes out to everyone when the gospel is preached. Consider verses 23–25: "You have been born again, not of perishable seed but of imperishable, through the living and abiding word of God." Notice: The new birth happens through the word of God. Verse 25 says that this word of God "is the good news that was preached to you."

However, the gospel is preached to all people, yet not all are born again. That's why we talk about a general call of God through the gospel. The general call—the preached word of God, the gospel—enters the ears of all the hearers who are spiritually dead. But not all live. Why do some live and have faith? Why do some of the blind see, and some of the deaf hear?

THE CALL CREATES WHAT IT COMMANDS

The answer is stated in many different ways in the New Testament. One is here in verse 23: Some are "born again...of incorruptible seed through the...gospel." The gospel is preached to all, and the divine seed is implanted in some. That's one way to say it. Another is to say that some are *called*. And this calling is not the same as the general call that all receive externally in the preaching of the gospel. Rather, it's the internal effective call of God's triumphant word of creation. It's the call of Jesus at the tomb of Lazarus. He says to a dead man: "Lazarus, come out" (John 11:43). And the call creates what it commands.

That's the difference between the external, general call that all hear when the gospel is preached and the internal, effective call. The internal call is God's sovereign, creative, unstoppable voice. It creates what it commands. God speaks not just to the ear and the mind, but he speaks to the heart. His internal heart-call opens the eyes of the blind heart, and opens the ears of the deaf heart, and causes Christ to appear as the supremely valuable person that he really is. So the heart freely and eagerly embraces Christ as the Treasure that he is. That's what God does when he calls us through the gospel (see 1 Pet. 2:9; 5:10).

Perhaps the clearest text of all about the unique power of God's internal, effective call is 1 Corinthians 1:22–24: "Jews demand signs and Greeks seek wisdom, but we preach Christ crucified, a stumbling block to Jews and folly to Gentiles, but to those who are called, both Jews and Greeks, Christ the power of God and the wisdom of God." All hear the gospel—Jews and Greeks. But some Jews and some Greeks experience something in the gospel: They stop seeing Christ as a stumbling block and as foolishness. Instead, they now see him as "the power of God and the wisdom of God." What happened? "To those who are called...he is Christ the power of God and the wisdom of God." The sovereign, creative call of God opened their eyes, and they saw Christ for the power and the wisdom that he is.

That is the third way that God causes us to be born again. 1) He ransomed us from sin and wrath by the blood of Christ and paid the debt for sinners to have eternal life. 2) He raised Jesus from the dead so that union with Jesus gives eternal life that never fades away. 3) He called us from darkness to light and from death to life through the gospel and gave us eyes to see and ears to hear. He made the light of the glory of God in the face of Christ shine in our hearts through the gospel. And we believed. We embraced Christ for the Treasure that he is.

ALL THINGS FOR GOOD

O that every believer would know the glory of what has happened to him! Do you know what God has done for you and in you? You were ransomed with the imperishable blood of Christ. You were raised with Christ from the dead to an eternally living hope. You were called from death to life like Lazarus, and you saw Christ for the Treasure that he is. You were born again. You received him and were saved.

Perhaps the next time you apply Romans 8:28 to a hardship in your life it will have new power because of what we have seen: "We know that for those who love God all things work together for good, for those who are called according to his purpose." If you are called—if you are born again—all things work for your good. All things. And if you are not yet born again, hear the call! Hear God's call in this gospel of Christ and believe. If you receive Christ for who he is, you will be saved from the wrath of God and he will work everything for your everlasting good.

Remind them to be submissive to rulers and authorities, to be obedient, to be ready for every good work, to speak evil of no one, to avoid quarreling, to be gentle, and to show perfect courtesy toward all people. For we ourselves were once foolish, disobedient, led astray, slaves to various passions and pleasures, passing our days in malice and envy, hated by others and hating one another. But when the goodness and loving kindness of God our Savior appeared, he saved us, not because of works done by us in righteousness, but according to his own mercy, by the washing of regeneration and renewal of the Holy Spirit, whom he poured out on us richly through Jesus Christ our Savior, so that being justified by his grace we might become heirs according to the hope of eternal life. The saying is trustworthy, and I want you to insist on these things, so that those who have believed in God may be careful to devote themselves to good works. These things are excellent and profitable for people.

Titus 3:1–8

7

Through the Washing of Regeneration

Notice the word *regeneration* in Titus 3:5: "He [that is, God] saved us, not because of works done by us in righteousness, but according to his own mercy, by the washing of *regeneration* and renewal of the Holy Spirit." *Regeneration* is another way of speaking about the *new birth* or the *second birth* or being *born again*.

We have discussed what the new birth is (Chapters 1–2), and why it is necessary (Chapters 3–5). Then in the previous chapter, we began to address how it happens. In this chapter, we continue that question: *How does God bring about the new birth?* But first, there are some very important new signals here about what it is and why we need it. Consider one of each.

A New Signal about What New Birth Is

Consider an unusual signal about what the new birth is. The word for *regeneration* in verse 5 ("[God] saved us...by the washing of *regeneration*" [*palingenesias*]) is used only one other place in the entire Bible, namely, Matthew 19:28. Jesus says to the twelve apostles, "Truly, I say to you, in *the new world* (a very loose translation of "in the regeneration" [*en tē palingenesia*]), when the Son of Man will sit on his glorious throne, you who have followed me will also sit on twelve thrones, judging the twelve tribes of Israel." This is a reference to the rebirth of the creation. It's like saying "…in the new heavens and the new earth" that Isaiah spoke about in Isaiah 65:17 and 66:22.

Jesus conceives of the new birth as something that will happen to all creation, not just human beings. Humans are not the only part of reality that is fallen and defiled and disordered. The whole creation is. Why is that? The answer is that when human beings sinned at the very beginning, God made all creation a visible display of the horrors of sin. Disease, degeneration, natural disasters—these are all part of the visual, audible, touchable images of the moral outrage that sin entered the world and pervades the world.

THE MATERIAL CREATION BORN AGAIN

The most important passage in the Bible about this is Romans 8:20–23. And it's important for this chapter because it confirms and clarifies what Jesus said about the creation undergoing a "new birth"—the "regeneration."

> The creation [All of it! Not just the people] was subjected to futility, not willingly, but because of him who subjected it, [namely, God, since only God can subject the creation to futility in hope] in hope that the creation itself will be set free from its bondage to corruption and obtain the freedom of the glory of the children of God. [There will be a great renewal someday and it will happen so that creation joins the children of God in their glorious renewal.] For we know that the whole creation has been groaning

together in the pains of childbirth until now. [There's the imagery of new birth, just like Jesus said.] And not only the creation, but we ourselves, who have the firstfruits of the Spirit, groan inwardly as we wait eagerly for adoption as sons, the redemption of our bodies.

So if we put it all together, the picture seems to be something like this: God's purpose is that the entire creation be born again. That is, the whole universe will replace its futility and corruption and disease and degeneration and disasters with a whole new order—a new heaven and a new earth. This will be the great, universal regeneration; the great, universal new birth.

When Paul uses this word (regeneration, *palingenesias*) in Titus 3:5, he wants us to see that our new birth is a part of that. The newness we have by virtue of our regeneration now is the firstfruits—the down payment and guarantee—of the greater newness we will have when our bodies are made new as a part of the universe being made new. Paul said in Romans 8:23, "We... who have the firstfruits of the Spirit [because we have been born again by the Spirit] groan inwardly as we wait eagerly for adoption as sons, the redemption of our bodies."

So when you think of your new birth, think of it as the first installment of what is coming. Your body and the whole world will one day take part in this regeneration. God's final purpose is not spiritually renewed souls inhabiting decrepit bodies in a disease- and disaster-ravaged world. His purpose is a renewed world with renewed bodies and renewed souls that take all our renewed senses and make them a means of enjoying and praising God.

When you hear the word *regeneration* in Titus 3:5, hear it that big. "[God] saved us, not because of works done by us in righteousness, but according to his own mercy, by the washing of regeneration and renewal of the Holy Spirit." When he says in verse 7 that the aim of the new birth is "that being justified by his grace we might become heirs according to the hope of eternal life," he means heirs of everything included in that eternal life—new heavens, new earth, new body, new perfected relationships, new sinless sight of all that is good and glorious, and new capacities for a kind of pleasure in God that will exceed all our dreams.

That's the new signal in Titus 3 of what the new birth is: It's the first installment of the final, universal regeneration of the universe.

A NEW SIGNAL ABOUT WHY WE NEED THE NEW BIRTH

Then there is a clear signal *why* we need this regeneration. It's found in Titus 3:3: "We ourselves were once foolish, disobedient, led astray, slaves to various passions and pleasures, passing our days in malice and envy, hated by others and hating one another." That is not a description of the material creation. That's a description of the human heart. Those are *moral* evils, not physical evils. Foolish. Disobedient. Led astray. Slaves to sinful pleasures. Malice. Envy. Hating. We are all in that list somewhere.

The reason we need regeneration is that God will not welcome such hearts into his new creation. As Jesus said, unless we are born again, we will not see the kingdom of God (John 3:3). This is why all of us must be born again. We must be changed.

THE MEANING OF GRACE: BUT GOD...

Then comes one of the most precious phrases in the Bible (v. 4): "*But...God.*" We were foolish, disobedient, led astray, slaves to sinful pleasures, malicious, envious, hated and hating. *But...God...* "*But* when the goodness and loving kindness of *God* appeared, he [God!] saved us."

This is the same amazing sequence that we saw in Ephesians 2:3–5: "[We were] carrying out the desires of the body and the mind, and were by nature children of wrath, like the rest of mankind. But God, being rich in mercy, because of the great love with which he loved us, even when we were dead in our trespasses, made us alive together with Christ—by grace you have been saved." We were dead, but God made us alive. This is the meaning of grace. The dead can do nothing to make themselves live. But God...

That's what we have here in Titus 3:3–5. We were slaves to desires and pleasures that were so powerful we could not taste and see that the Lord was good. So far as our ability to know and trust and love God was concerned, we were dead. But... God. Verses 4–5: "But when the goodness and loving kindness of God our Savior appeared, he saved us, not because of works done by us in righteousness, but according to his own mercy, by the washing of regeneration and renewal of the Holy Spirit."

How? By Washing and Renewal

So we turn now to the third question: *How* does God do it? How does the new birth happen? Just as we saw in the words of Jesus in John 3, Paul describes regeneration as a *cleansing* and a *renewing*. At the end of Titus 3:5, Paul says that God saved us "by the *washing* of regeneration and *renewal* of the Holy Spirit." Regeneration is a kind of *washing*. And regeneration is a kind of *renewal*.

Recall that Jesus said in John 3:5, "Unless one is born of water and the Spirit, he cannot enter the kingdom of God." Notice the parallel thought in Titus 3:5: You were saved by the washing of regeneration and renewal of the Holy Spirit.

My argument in Chapter 2 concerning John 3 was that this language of water and Spirit came from Ezekiel 36:25–27 where God promises his people,

> I will sprinkle clean water on you, and you shall be clean from all your uncleannesses, and from all your idols I will cleanse you. And I will give you a new heart, and a new spirit I will put within you....And I will put my Spirit within you, and cause you to walk in my statutes.

Jesus was saying something like this: "The time of the New Covenant promises has arrived. Ezekiel's promise is coming to pass by the Spirit in connection with me. The Spirit gives life (John 6:63). And I am the way, the truth, and the life (John 14:6). And when the Spirit connects you to me by faith, you experience a new birth. And there are at least two ways to look at it: *cleansing* from all that is past and *renewal* for all that is future."

So when Paul says here in Titus 3:5 that God "saved us...by the washing of regeneration and renewal of the Holy Spirit," he means roughly the same thing as Jesus did: The promises of the New Covenant have arrived. The beginning of the kingdom of God is here. The final universal "regeneration" has begun. And your new birth is a cleansing from all the sin that you have ever committed. It is also the creation of a new nature by the Holy Spirit. You are still you after the new birth. But there are two changes: You are clean, and you are new. That is what it means to be born again, regenerated.

How did God bring that about? What Paul wants to emphasize here is that it is owing to the way God is, not owing to what we have done—even done in righteousness. Verses 4–5 give three descriptions of the way God is and put this in contrast to anything we might try to do to be born again. "But when the goodness and loving kindness of God our Savior appeared, he saved us, not because of works done by us in righteousness, but according to his own mercy, by the washing of regeneration and renewal of the Holy Spirit."

Salvation is the big overarching idea in this text ("he saved us," v. 5). But the specific way he does it is regeneration. And Paul traces both of them back to God's "goodness," his "loving kindness" (v. 4), and his "mercy" (v. 5). This is Paul's ultimate answer to how God regenerates sinners. God is good. God is loving. God is merciful.

BY THE KINDNESS OF GOD

If you are born again—if you were wakened from spiritual death, and given eyes to see, and ears to hear, and a spiritual sense to taste that Jesus is supremely satisfying, and a heart to trust him—it is owing to the kindness of God. The key first word in verse 4 (*chrēstotēs*) means *kindness* or *goodness*. Paul uses it in Ephesians 2:7: "[God made us alive] so that in the coming ages he might show the immeasurable riches of his grace in *kindness* toward us in Christ Jesus."

God loves to lavish kindness on us. The bigger your conception of God, the more amazing this is. God is the creator of the universe. He holds the galaxies in being. He governs everything that happens in the world, down to the fall of a bird and the number of your hairs (Matt. 10:29–30). He is infinitely strong and wise and holy and just. And amazingly, he is kind. "When the kindness of God appeared..." (Titus 3:4). And because of this kindness, we were born again. Let your very existence as a Christian tell you every hour of every day: God is kind to you.

BY THE PHILANTHROPY OF GOD

The second way Paul describes God's nature which gives rise to his regenerating us is translated in the ESV "loving kindness." The Greek word is *philanthrōpia*, from which we get our word *philanthropy*: love of humanity. This is not a common word in the Bible for God's love. In fact, it occurs only here in the New Testament. Paul says that God's heart inclines to do humanity good. He is in the highest sense a philanthropist. So Paul is saying, if you are born again, it happened because of God's inclination to bless humanity.

Then he says something absolutely essential and Christ-exalting. He says in verse 4 that this kindness and this humanity-blessing inclination "appeared." "But when the goodness and loving kindness of God our Savior appeared, he saved us...through the washing of regeneration." What does that mean? The kindness and love of God appeared. It means that if they simply stay there in the being of God and don't come down and take human form among us, they would save nobody.

How did they appear? How did the kindness and love of God appear? The answer is found in noticing the fact that God is called "our Savior" in verse 4 ("the kindness of God our Savior appeared"). And Jesus is called "our Savior" in verse 6: "Whom [that is, the Spirit] he [God] poured out on us richly through Jesus Christ our Savior." In other words, God "our Savior" appeared in the person of Christ "our Savior." Jesus himself is the appearing of the goodness and love of God.

This means that our regeneration is owing to the historical work of Christ. We have seen this repeatedly in this book. New birth is not a vague spiritual change disconnected from history. It is an objective historical act of the Spirit of God connecting us by faith to the historical, incarnate—the appearing—Lord Jesus, so that the life he now has as the crucified and risen Savior has become our life because we are united to him. New birth happens because Jesus came into the world as the kindness and love of God and died for sins and rose again.

By the Mercy of God, Not Our Deeds

The third aspect of God's nature that explains our new birth is his mercy. Paul mentions it in a way to make clear that we should contrast God's mercy with our own deeds as the basis for how regeneration happens. Verse 5: "He saved us, *not because of works done by us in righteousness*, but *according to his own mercy*, by the washing of regeneration."

If you are born again, you owe it to the mercy of God. God is merciful. We didn't deserve to be born again. We were hard and resistant and spiritually dead. God would have been righteous to pass us by. "But God, being rich in mercy...even when we were dead in our trespasses, made us alive together with Christ" (Eph. 2:4–5). We owe our new life—our new birth—to mercy.

Not Our Best Works and Best Motives

God is kind. God is loving toward humanity. God is merciful. That is how we were born again. God did it. Paul could have left it like that. Only positive statements. But he didn't. He was burdened to negate something. He said in verse 5, "He saved us, *not because of works done by us in righteousness*." He knows our tendencies. We tend to think that if something good happens to us, it must be because we did something good. Paul knows this about us. And he warns us against it.

When it comes to salvation through the new birth, don't think that way. Notice carefully, he does not say: This salvation was not owing to works done in legalism. He says: This salvation— this new birth—is not owing to works done in righteousness. Not only your worst works and worst motives, but even your best works and best motives are excluded. They didn't make you regenerate; they don't cause you to stay regenerate. It's the other way around. Staying regenerate causes them.

This is one reason why I do not think the "washing of regeneration" in verse 5 refers to baptism. Whether circumcision in the Old Covenant or baptism in the New Covenant—it is not good things we do, not even sacraments, that cause us to be born again. The kindness of God. The love of God. The absolutely free mercy of God. These explain our new birth. Not circumcision. Not baptism. Not any works done by us in righteousness. New birth comes and brings righteous deeds with it—not the other way around.

May God give you eyes to see that nothing could make you humbler and nothing could make you happier than the truth that you have been born again, not because of anything you did, but because of the mercy of God. Submit to that, and be glad.

Therefore, preparing your minds for action, and being sober-minded, set your hope fully on the grace that will be brought to you at the revelation of Jesus Christ. As obedient children, do not be conformed to the passions of your former ignorance, but as he who called you is holy, you also be holy in all your conduct, since it is written, "You shall be holy, for I am holy." And if you call on him as Father who judges impartially according to each one's deeds, conduct yourselves with fear throughout the time of your exile, knowing that you were ransomed from the futile ways inherited from your forefathers, not with perishable things such as silver or gold, but with the precious blood of Christ, like that of a lamb without blemish or spot. He was foreknown before the foundation of the world but was made manifest in the last times for the sake of you who through him are believers in God, who raised him from the dead and gave him glory, so that your faith and hope are in God. Having purified your souls by your obedience to the truth for a sincere brotherly love, love one another earnestly from a pure heart, since you have been born again, not of perishable seed but of imperishable, through the living and abiding word of God; for "All flesh is like grass and all its glory like the flower of grass. The grass withers, and the flower falls, but the word of the Lord remains forever." And this word is the good news that was preached to you.

1 Peter 1:13–25

8

THROUGH FAITH IN JESUS CHRIST

Just before writing this book, I read the autobiography of Supreme Court Justice Clarence Thomas, *My Grandfather's Son: A Memoir*. He had been raised as a Roman Catholic and attended Holy Cross College in Worcester, Massachusetts. But while there, he parted ways with the church, though not forever. Here is what he said:

> During my second week on campus, I went to Mass for the first and last time at Holy Cross. I don't know why I bothered—probably habit, or guilt—but whatever the reasons, I got up and walked out midway through the homily. It was all about Church dogma, not the social problems with which I was obsessed, and seemed to me hopelessly irrelevant.[13]

WHAT IS RELEVANCE?

As a preacher, I think a lot about relevance. Why should anyone listen to what I have to say? Why should anybody care? *Relevance*

13 Clarence Thomas, *My Grandfather's Son: A Memoir* (New York: HarperCollins, 2007), 51.

is an ambiguous word. It might mean that a sermon is relevant if it *feels* to the listeners that it will make a significant difference in their lives. Or it might mean that a sermon is relevant if it *will* make a significant difference in their lives whether they feel it or not.

That second kind of relevance is what guides my sermons and my writing. In other words, I want to say things that are really significant for your life whether you know they are or not. My way of doing that is to stay as close as I can to what God says is important in his word, not what we think is important apart from God's word.

So in any given worship service a dozen young, idealistic Clarence Thomases might be present, full of anger about racism, or global warming, or abortion, or limited health care for children, or homelessness, or poverty, or the war in Iraq, or white-collar crime, or human trafficking, or the global AIDS crisis, or rampant fatherlessness, or the greed behind the sub-prime mortgage crisis, or the treatment of illegal aliens, or the plight of Christians just coming out of prison. And then they hear me announce that today we are going to talk about the way a person can be born again. And they might react like Clarence Thomas did and simply walk out and say, "That has nothing to do with the real problems this world is facing."

DEALING WITH WHAT MATTERS MOST

They would be wrong—doubly wrong. They would be wrong, in the first place, in failing to see that what Jesus meant by the new birth is supremely relevant for racism and global warming and abortion and health care and all the other issues of our day. We will see in the coming chapters what the necessary fruit of the new birth looks like.

And they would be wrong, secondly, in thinking that those issues are the most important issues in life. They aren't. They are life-and-death issues. But they are not the most important, because they deal with the relief of suffering during this brief earthly life, not the relief of suffering during the eternity that follows. Or to put it positively, they deal with how to maximize well-being now for eighty years or so, but not with how to maximize well-being in the presence of God for eighty trillion years and more.

My job as a pastor is to deal in what matters most, and to stay close to the revealed will of God in the Bible (so you can see it for yourselves), and to pray that, by God's grace, the young, idealistic, angry Clarence Thomases in the crowd, and everyone else, will see and feel the magnitude of what *God* says is important.

SEEING AND SAVORING THE MAGNIFICENCE OF JESUS

Jesus says in John 3:3, "Truly, truly, I say to you, unless one is born again he cannot see the kingdom of God." Not to see the kingdom of God is to be excluded from the kingdom of God. Jesus said in Matthew 8:11–12 that outside the kingdom is "outer darkness. In that place there will be weeping and gnashing of teeth." He called it "eternal punishment" (Matt. 25:46). The alternative to that is to be in the kingdom of God and spend eternity in everlasting joy with the greatest person in the universe (John 18:24).

Nothing is more important than the glory of Christ personally seen and savored in the kingdom of God with all the countless number who have believed in his name. That glory will one day fill the earth with peace and justice and everything good. Christ himself will be the center and radiant through it all.

WHAT IS OUR INVOLVEMENT IN THE NEW BIRTH?

The question in this chapter is: *What is our involvement?* What do we do in the act of new birth? How are we involved in it? Let me give you the answer first that I see in the Bible, and then I will try to show where it's found.

Your involvement in the event of the new birth is to exercise faith—faith in the crucified and risen Son of God, Jesus Christ, as the Savior and Lord and Treasure of your life. The way you are engaged in the event of your new birth is by believing on Christ. You are involved in the new birth because in it you receive Christ for who he really is, the supremely valuable Savior, Lord, and Treasure of the universe.

The answer continues like this: Your act of believing and God's act of begetting are simultaneous. He does the begetting and you do the believing at the same instant. And—this is very important—his doing is the decisive cause of your doing. His begetting is the decisive cause of your believing.

If you have a hard time thinking of one thing causing another thing if they are simultaneous, think of fire and heat or fire and light. The instant there is fire, there is heat. The instant there is fire, there is light. But we would not say that the heat caused the fire, or the light caused the fire. We say that the fire caused the heat and the light.

That's the answer I see in the Bible to the question *How are we involved in the new birth?* Now we will look at some passages of Scripture that direct me to these thoughts.

"OBEDIENCE TO THE TRUTH"

We will start here in 1 Peter 1:22–23:

> Having purified your souls by your obedience to the truth for a sincere brotherly love, love one another earnestly from a pure heart, since you have been born again, not of perishable seed but of imperishable, through the living and abiding word of God.

Notice several things here. One is that the aim of what is happening is love. "Having purified your souls by your obedience to the truth for a sincere brotherly love." In other words, the purification of the soul by obedience to the truth is leading somewhere, namely, to a sincere brotherly love. One of the implications of seeing this is that the purifying of the soul is not itself the presence of brotherly love—not yet. The purifying of the soul is "for brotherly love." It is "to the end of brotherly love." Love is a very basic fruit of the Spirit. So verse 22 means that something more basic than brotherly love is happening when it says "having purified your souls by your obedience to the truth."

"Obedience" here is, therefore, not the obedience of love. It leads to the obedience of love. What is it then? Obedience to the truth is the right response to "the truth." It is called the "obedience to the truth" (v. 22). And what is that truth? In this context, "the truth" refers to the word of God. That's what it's called in verse 23 ("through the living and abiding word of God"). And that word of God in verse 25 is called the good news, the gospel: "This word is the good news that was preached to you." So obeying the truth in verse 22 means obeying the gospel.

And what does obeying the gospel mean? It means believing in Jesus, because what the free offer of the gospel calls for is faith: "Believe on the Lord Jesus and you will be saved" (Acts 16:31; 1 Cor. 15:1–2). The first and basic command of the gospel is not "love your brother." What the gospel requires first is faith. So obeying the gospel at this basic level is having faith.

You can see this again in the third chapter of this letter. Husbands without faith in Christ are described as disobeying the word. "Likewise, wives, be subject to your own husbands, so that even if some do not obey the word, they may be won without a word" (1 Pet. 3:1). Not obeying the word means they are not believers. The same thing turns up in 1 Peter 2:8 ("they disobey the word") and 4:17 ("who do not obey the gospel of God"). So, not obeying the word means not obeying the gospel, that is, not believing.

Paul spoke the same way in 2 Thessalonians 1:8, where he said that God will inflict "vengeance on those who do not know God and on those who do not obey the gospel of our Lord Jesus." In other words, the gospel of the Lord Jesus calls for faith, and these people did not obey. They did not believe. They rejected "the word of truth, the gospel."[14]

So when Peter says that you have "purified your souls by your obedience to the truth for a sincere brotherly love" (1 Pet. 1:22), he means "you have purified your souls by faith in the gospel of Jesus Christ and this faith leads to brotherly love." Faith works through love (Gal. 5:6). Love comes from sincere faith (1 Tim. 1:5).

BELIEVING: ACTING OUT THE NEW BIRTH

Recall from the previous chapter that in John 3:5 and Titus 3:5 the new birth involves *purifying*—the imagery of water and washing. Jesus said, "Truly, truly, I say to you, unless one is born of *water* and the Spirit, he cannot enter the kingdom of God." And Paul said that God "saved us...by the *washing* of regeneration." So when Peter says that our souls have been *purified* by obedience to the truth—that is, by faith in the gospel—and says that this purification *leads* to love, and is not the same as love, I take him to mean that this purification is the purification which takes place in the new birth. It's the purification referred to in the "water" of John 3:5 and the "washing" of Titus 3:5. This is the new birth.

---

14 Ephesians 1:13: "In him you also, when you heard *the word of truth, the gospel* of your salvation, and believed in him, were sealed with the promised Holy Spirit." Colossians 1:5: "Of this you have heard before in *the word of the truth, the gospel.*"

Which means that the new birth in which we are washed, and the purification "by obedience to the truth," are part and parcel of the same event. We are, therefore, integrally involved in the new birth. It is *our* new birth. It involves our believing in the gospel of Jesus Christ. That's why I say that my new birth does not take place without me believing. In believing we are acting out the new birth, we are breathing in the new life.

GOD'S BEGETTING CAUSES OUR BELIEVING

Now in verse 23, Peter explains this in the very language of being born again. Let's put both verses together so you can see the connection between purifying the soul (our act) and being born again (God's act): "Having purified your souls by your obedience to the truth for a sincere brotherly love, love one another earnestly from a pure heart, since you have been born again not of perishable seed but of imperishable, through the living and abiding word of God." The connection between our action in the new birth (v. 22) and God's action in the new birth (v. 23) is a relationship of effect and cause. That's implied in the words "*since* [or because] you have been born again."[15] God's action is underneath our action. We purify our hearts in obedience to the gospel, that is, we act out regeneration; and we are able to do that because God regenerates us.

GOD IS THE DECISIVE CAUSE

There are three clues in this text that God's action in the new birth is the cause of our action in the new birth. That is, his begetting causes our believing.

15 Literally there is simply a participial connection between our purifying and God's giving birth (*anagegennēmenoi*, "having been born again," 1 Peter 1:23), but contextually it is clear that this participle is functioning as a ground or a cause of what went before.

First is simply the order of the statements. Verse 22 contains a command: "Love one another earnestly from a pure heart." And verse 22 contains a prerequisite to that love, namely, that we have purified our hearts by faith in the gospel. Then coming last, as it does, verse 23 seems to be a prerequisite of both of these. Because of God's work in begetting, you are able to believe the gospel, which purifies your heart, and then love each other. So God's begetting is underneath our believing and loving. It makes the believing and loving possible.

The second clue that God's begetting is the cause of our believing is that God makes the word the instrument of the new birth in verse 23: "You have been born again, not of perishable seed but of imperishable, through the living and abiding word of God." Some take the imperishable seed of verse 23 to be the Holy Spirit, and it may well be (see 1 John 3:9). But I'm inclined to take "the imperishable seed" to be "the word of God." The seed is described as "imperishable," and the word is described as "living and abiding." Those are virtually the same. So I take "born…of imperishable seed" to be synonymous with "[born] through the living and abiding word." This is confirmed by the fact that in verses 24–25 the entire focus is on the word, not the Spirit.

So the point is that God makes the word his instrument in the new birth, and the way the word works in the new birth is by awakening faith. That's what Paul says in Romans 10:17: "Faith comes from hearing, and hearing through the word of Christ." So if new birth involves our believing, and if the word causes our believing, and 1 Peter 1:24 says that God causes the new birth "through the word," then behind the word and behind our believing is the decisive work of God. This is what James says in James 1:18: "Of his own will he brought us forth by the word of truth." He brought us forth of his own will. God was not constrained by our will to believe. Ours was made possible by his.

The third clue related to this text that God's begetting is the cause of our believing is the way Peter uses this same language at the Jerusalem council in Acts 15. He says that Gentiles and Jews are both being saved, not just Jews. And the way he says it is significant: "[God] made no distinction between us and them, having cleansed their hearts by faith" (Acts 15:9).

Here he speaks the same way he does in 1 Peter 1:22, where he says, "Having purified your souls by your obedience to the truth..." That is, "having purified your souls by faith..." But in Acts 15:9 he uses the same language of purifying and faith but says explicitly that God does the purifying through our faith. "[God] made no distinction between us and them, having cleansed their hearts by faith." God cleansed their hearts through their faith. This shows us that in the new birth our faith is both a crucial aspect and an essential instrument of the purification which God effects in us. But it is not ultimate. It is not its own cause. God is.

WHAT THIS MEANS FOR US

What then does this mean for us? It means four things, and I pray you will receive them with joy.

1 It means we must believe in order to be saved. "Believe on the Lord Jesus Christ and you will be saved" (Acts 16:31). The new birth does not take the place of faith; the new birth involves faith. The new birth is the birth of faith.

2 It means that left to ourselves we will not believe. There is no hope that the dead will breathe by themselves.

3 It means that God, who is rich in mercy and great love and sovereign grace, is the decisive cause of your faith.

4 According to 1 Peter 1:22, the fruit of the born-again heart is love. Which means that nothing in life is untouched by

the new birth: racism, global warming, abortion, limited health care for children, homelessness, poverty, the war in Iraq, white-collar crime, human trafficking, the global AIDS crisis, rampant fatherlessness, the greed behind the sub-prime mortgage crisis, the treatment of illegal aliens, or the plight of Christians just coming out of prison. Nothing is untouched. And most important, you enter the kingdom of God and see the face of Jesus forever.

Therefore, I plead with you on behalf of Christ, believe on the Lord Jesus Christ. Receive him as the Savior and Lord and Treasure of your life. If you are a believer already, humble yourself under the gracious hand of God, and as an everlasting, invincible child of God, give yourself to relieving suffering, especially eternal suffering. Help the young Clarence Thomases among us to see the connection between truth and love—between gospel regeneration and gospel liberation.

In the beginning was the Word, and the Word was with God, and the Word was God. He was in the beginning with God. All things were made through him, and without him was not any thing made that was made. In him was life, and the life was the light of men. The light shines in the darkness, and the darkness has not overcome it. There was a man sent from God, whose name was John. He came as a witness, to bear witness about the light, that all might believe through him. He was not the light, but came to bear witness about the light. The true light, which enlightens everyone, was coming into the world. He was in the world, and the world was made through him, yet the world did not know him. He came to his own, and his own people did not receive him. But to all who did receive him, who believed in his name, he gave the right to become children of God, who were born, not of blood nor of the will of the flesh nor of the will of man, but of God. And the Word became flesh and dwelt among us, and we have seen his glory, glory as of the only Son from the Father, full of grace and truth.

John 1:1–14

9

THROUGH INTELLIGIBLE GOOD NEWS

Recently I was listening to a recording of Vishal Mangalwadi's lecture "From Bach to Cobain," which is part of a series that he gave at the University of Minnesota under the title "Must the Sun Set on the West?" In this lecture, he spoke briefly about the use of the mantra in Eastern religions. When I heard what he said, I thought: That will be very significant in helping me make one of my points in this chapter, namely, how the "word" functions to bring about the new birth.

So let me try to make a connection between the focus of the previous chapter on 1 Peter 1:23 and the present focus on John 1:12–13 by means of pondering how a mantra differs from the gospel. It is amazing how many religious websites link the meaning of mantra to John 1:1: "In the beginning was the Word, and the Word was with God, and the Word was God." The point they make is that reality is essentially sound, and we can gain access to ultimate reality by repeating certain sacred sounds. Hence, mantra.

Verbal Sounds without Verbal Meaning

One website explains a mantra like this: "Just by repeating the name, that which cannot be understood will be understood, and just by repeating the name that which cannot be seen, will be seen."[16] In other words, the way a mantra works is not by clarifying the meaning of words and showing how the meaning of words corresponds to reality. Rather, a mantra is a combination of verbal sounds without verbal meaning. The aim of a mantra is not to make ideas clear, but to make ideas vanish, so that there is a more immediate access to ultimate reality.

Knowing where you stand in this matter is very important. Some Christians, who don't know what they believe about how God relates to us through the mind, lose their bearings and drift into the practices of Eastern religions without any sense that they may be cutting themselves off from Christ.

An Intelligible Narration about Jesus

1 Peter 1:23 says, as we saw in the last chapter, that we "have been born again, not of perishable seed but of imperishable, *through the living and abiding word of God.*" This sentence is stupendously important. We are born again, that is, we are united by the Holy Spirit to Jesus Christ so that we share in his new, eternal resurrection life *through the word of God.* This miracle, this transfer from death to life, happens through the hearing of the word of God.

Now you need to decide whether you think this is a reference to the use of the word of God as a mantra, or the use of the word of God as a mentally intelligible narration of real historical events concerning Jesus Christ and what this person and these events mean for those who believe. Are we connected to divine reality—to God

---

16 www.meditationiseasy.com/mCorner/techniques/Mantra_meditation.htm, accessed 05-01-08.

in the new birth—by the mystical processes of repetition of sacred sounds, freeing our minds from thought, and gaining immediate access to ultimate reality, or are we connected to divine reality—to Jesus Christ crucified and risen—by hearing and believing the intelligible words of God as the narration of what Jesus Christ accomplished for us when he died and rose again in history?

After saying in 1 Peter 1:23 that we are born again "through the living and abiding word of God," Peter says in verse 25, "This word is the good news that was preached to you." In other words, the word through which we are born again is "the good news that was preached to you." And what is that? What is that gospel or good news? It's this:

> Now I would remind you, brothers, of the gospel I preached to you, which you received, in which you stand, and by which you are being saved, if you hold fast to the word I preached to you—unless you believed in vain. For I delivered to you as of first importance what I also received: that Christ died for our sins in accordance with the Scriptures, that he was buried, that he was raised on the third day in accordance with the Scriptures, and that he appeared to Cephas, then to the twelve. (1 Cor. 15:1–5)

THE GOSPEL IS NEWS

In other words, the gospel is news about events and their significance. It's about events that happened, that people could see with their eyes and touch with their hands and think about with their minds and describe with their mouths. It's the news about the death of Jesus in history and his resurrection and these events getting their meaning, as Paul says, from Scripture: "Christ died for our sins *in accordance with the Scriptures.*"

We are saved, Paul says in 1 Corinthians 15:2, by believing this news. And we believe it because we heard it and understood it with our minds. Paul ends that section in 1 Corinthians 15:11

by saying, "So we preach and so you believed." As he said in Romans 10:17: "Faith comes from hearing, and hearing through the word of Christ." And Galatians 3:2, 5: "Did you receive the Spirit by works of the law or by hearing with faith?...Does he who supplies the Spirit to you and works miracles among you do so by works of the law, or by hearing with faith?"

In other words, "hearing with faith" is what happens when we are "born again through the living and abiding word of God." The gospel—the news about Jesus Christ—is preached, we hear it, and through it we are born again. Faith is brought into being. "Of his own will he brought us forth by the word of truth" (James 1:18).

IT DOESN'T WORK LIKE THAT

This truth, this living and abiding word, this gospel, is not a mantra. And it doesn't work like a mantra. It doesn't work through the repetition of sacred sounds. It works because it is the intelligible truth about what really happened when Jesus died and rose again, and because God means for his Son to be glorified by our knowing and believing who his Son really is and what he really did to save sinners.

What we learn from 1 Peter 1:23 ("born again through the living and abiding word of God, the gospel") is that the whole worldview supporting the mantra is misguided and mistaken. It isn't rooted in history. It isn't rooted in Jesus Christ. It isn't rooted in the intelligibility of historical narrative. It isn't rooted in the responsibility of the human mind to construe meaning from the preaching of Christ. It isn't rooted in the duty of the soul to see and believe the gospel of Christ crucified and risen.

O how jealous I am that the followers of Jesus be a Christ-exalting, Bible-saturated, discerning people. For example, I pray that you don't just sign up for your local yoga class and not know what you are doing. Yoga is to the body what mantra is to the mouth. The two are rooted in the same worldview. Take my own town as an example. When I go to the Minneapolis YWCA website and click on "fitness classes," I find 22 references to yoga, including Beginning Yoga, MS Yoga, Youngster Yoga, Youth Dance and Yoga, and Yoga for Everybody.

One explanation says that in "mantra yoga" one "has to chant a word or a phrase until he/she transcends mind and emotions. In the process the super conscious is discovered and achieved."[17] Then yoga itself is described like this:

> Yoga focuses on harmony between mind and body. Yoga derives its philosophy from Indian metaphysical beliefs. The word yoga comes from the Sanskrit language and means union or merger. The ultimate aim of this philosophy is to strike a balance between mind and body and attain self-enlightenment. To achieve this, yoga uses movement, breath, posture, relaxation, and meditation in order to establish a healthy, lively, and balanced approach to life.[18]

You were born again through the living and abiding word of God. This word is the gospel of Jesus Christ crucified and risen. Don't fall prey to another gospel. There is no other gospel, and there is no other path to God—or to ultimate well-being—than hearing, understanding, and believing the scandalous news of Jesus Christ in the gospel.

THE WORD BECAME FLESH

So when we come to John 1:1 ("In the beginning was the Word, and the Word was with God, and the Word was God"), we will not stop there, tear it out of its context, and fit it into a worldview that tries to transcend the flesh with meditation, mantras, and

17 http://yoga.iloveindia.com/yoga-types/mantra-yoga.html, accessed 5-1-08.
18 http://yoga.iloveindia.com/what-yoga.html, accessed 05-01-08.

yoga. No, we will read all the way to verse 14 and beyond: "And the Word *became flesh and dwelt among us*, and we have seen his glory, glory as of the only Son from the Father, full of grace and truth."

This is why the word through which we are born again cannot be a mantra. It became flesh and dwelt among us and lived a perfect life and died in our place and bore the wrath of God and rose physically from the dead, and it now comes to us in a historical narrative called *the gospel*. The Word was God and is God. He was not a sound. He was a Person. He was called the Word because he represents the expression of all that God the Father is.

And the Word became flesh. And the story of his saving work—the gospel, the word of God—is the way Jesus Christ, the Word, comes to us and regenerates us and renews us. We hear this word, and by grace, we understand this word, and receive this word, and are born again by this word. And we never, never, never try—by mantras or any other means—to empty our minds of this word. Never.

Born Not of Man but of God

Focus briefly on John 1:11–13:

> He came to his own, and his own people did not receive him. But to all who did receive him, who believed in his name, he gave the right to become children of God, who were born, not of blood nor of the will of the flesh nor of the will of man, but of God.

This text has the same structure as 1 Peter 1:22–23, which we have spent so much time on. In verse 12, those who are given the right to be the children of God are those who *receive* Christ and *believe* on his name. So being a child of God is connected to believing. It doesn't say how it's connected—which causes which—it just says they are connected. If you receive Christ, if you believe in his name, you are a child of God. That is, you are born again and belong to God's family forever. So becoming a child of God is connected to our act of believing. That's like 1 Peter 1:22.

Then in John 1:13, being born again is connected not with our act of believing but with God's act of begetting: "...who were born, not of blood nor of the will of the flesh nor of the will of man, but of God." The emphasis in verse 13 is to make clear that the act of the new birth is not caused by ordinary human agency.

There are three negations: not of blood (literally "bloods"), not of the will of the flesh, not of the will of man (literally, of a male, that is, a husband). In other words, the emphasis falls on saying that being in God's family is decisively not connected with being in any human family—including the Jewish family. Being born the second time does not depend on who gave birth to you the first time.

"Not of bloods" means that two people coming together from two bloodlines is irrelevant. Their union does not make a child of God. "Not of the will of the flesh" means that humanity as mere humanity (flesh) cannot produce a child of God. Jesus says in John 3:6, "That which is born of the flesh is flesh." That's all that flesh can produce. It can't produce a child of God. "Not of the will of a male" means that no husband, no matter how holy he is, can produce a child of God.

The alternative to all these is not any human act, but God himself. Verse 13: "...who were born, not of blood nor of the will of the flesh nor of the will of man, but of God." Decisive over human blood and human will and human husbands is God. Those who received Christ and believed on his name are born of God. They are the born-again ones.

The emphasis of John 1:12–13 falls on new birth being the work of God, not man. So how does John understand the relationship between our act of believing and God's act of begetting? Does God's begetting cause our believing, or does our believing bring about God's begetting? Does the new birth bring about faith, or does faith bring about the new birth? If we only had these verses, the emphasis would fall on: not of the will of the flesh, but of God. That is, God's begetting, not man's believing would appear to be decisive in the new birth.

God's Begetting Causes Our Believing

But we are not limited to these verses to know what John teaches about how our faith and God's work in the new birth relate to each other. John tells us plainly in 1 John 5:1. This is the clearest text in the New Testament on the relationship between faith and the new birth. Watch the verbs closely as we read 1 John 5:1: "Everyone who *believes* that Jesus is the Christ *has been born of God.*" Here is what John Stott says on this verse, and I agree totally:

> The combination of present tense (believes) and perfect tense [has been born] is important. It shows clearly that believing is the consequence, not the cause, of the new birth. Our present, continuing activity of believing is the result, and therefore, the evidence, of our past experience of new birth by which we became and remain God's children.[19]

So here's the upshot of these last two chapters: God's act in bringing about the new birth is the bringing into being of a *believer* where once there was only spiritual deadness and unbelief. The reason that the new birth is God's creation of a

19 John Stott, *The Letters of John* (Grand Rapids, MI: Eerdmans, 1988), 175.

believer is that this new creation happens *through the word of God* (1 Pet. 1:23; James 1:18)—through the gospel. The gospel of Jesus Christ, by the power of the Spirit, creates spiritual understanding and faith where once there was blindness and unbelief.[20] It does this as a narrative of historical events—the cross and the resurrection—that reveal the glory of Jesus Christ (2 Cor. 4:4–6). This narrative is the power of God bringing about the new birth and awakening faith (Rom. 1:16).

Therefore, the new birth does not come through a mantra or anything like it. It comes as a God-given, clear-headed, conscious embrace of the historical person Jesus Christ as the Savior, Lord, and Treasure of our life. And because of that I can—and I do—appeal to you: Look at him in the gospel—the story of his life and death and resurrection and what they mean for your life. See his glory and his truth. Receive him and believe in his name. And you will be a child of God.

---

20 For more on faith as a gift of God, see 2 Tim. 2:25–26; Eph. 2:8; Phil. 1:29; Acts 5:31; 13:48; 16:14; 18:27.

PART FOUR

WHAT ARE THE EFFECTS OF THE NEW BIRTH?

Everyone who believes that Jesus is the Christ has been born of God, and everyone who loves the Father loves whoever has been born of him. By this we know that we love the children of God, when we love God and obey his commandments. For this is the love of God, that we keep his commandments. And his commandments are not burdensome. For everyone who has been born of God overcomes the world. And this is the victory that has overcome the world—our faith. Who is it that overcomes the world except the one who believes that Jesus is the Son of God?

1 John 5:1–5

10

IT OVERCOMES THE WORLD

We turn now from the *What?* and *Why?* and *How?* questions to the effects or the evidences of the new birth. We ask where the new birth leads. What fruit does it produce in our lives? *What are the signs in your life that God has caused you to be born again?*

Now to focus on the effects of the new birth, we turn to the book of the Bible that is almost totally devoted to answering this question, namely, the First Epistle of John. I have a 100-year-old commentary on 1 John in my library called *The Tests of Life* by Robert Law.[21] It's a good title. What it means is that John wrote this letter to provide the church with tests or criteria for knowing if we have spiritual life, that is, if we have been born again.

To encourage you to read through 1 John for yourself, let me give you an overview of what I mean in saying that 1 John is written to help you know you have been born again. This chapter is an overview of 1 John, with a brief look at 1 John 5:3–4. The

---

21 Robert Law, *The Tests of Life: A Study of the First Epistle of John* (Grand Rapids, MI: Baker Book House, orig. 1909).

impact of the book as a whole has been for me very significant. I hope it may be for you.

Why Did John Write This Letter?

First, why did John write this letter? He gives his reason for writing in different ways. Let's take them in the order that they come.

> 1 John 1:4: "We are writing these things so that our joy may be complete." John is an unashamed Christian Hedonist.[22] The joy of their assurance will be his joy. And he wants it. It is good to want that kind of joy.

> 1 John 2:1: "My little children, I am writing these things to you so that you may not sin. But if anyone does sin, we have an advocate with the Father, Jesus Christ the righteous." He hopes his book will give them fresh power to overcome sin. And part of his method in helping them overcome sin is to assure them that failures do not have to prove fatal to your eternal life.

> 1 John 2:12–13: "I am writing to you, little children, because your sins are forgiven for his name's sake. I am writing to you, fathers, because you know him who is from the beginning. I am writing to you, young men, because you have overcome the evil one." In other words, he is filled with hope that the ones he is writing to are truly believers. They are forgiven. They do know God. They have triumphed over the evil one.

> 1 John 2:21: "I write to you, not because you do not know the truth, but because you know it, and because no lie is

22 Christian Hedonism teaches that the value of God shines more brightly in the soul that finds deepest satisfaction in him. Christian Hedonism, as I understand it, is most fully developed in John Piper, *Desiring God: Meditations of the Christian Hedonist*, 3rd ed. (Sisters, Ore.: Multnomah, 2003).

of the truth." This letter is not to get you started in the Christian life, but to confirm you in it.

1 John 2:26: "I write these things to you about those who are trying to deceive you." He is concerned with false teaching. This letter is meant to protect them from those who would lead them astray. In other words, the fact that we are born again does not mean we no longer need warnings.

1 John 5:13: "I write these things to you who believe in the name of the Son of God that you may know that you have eternal life." This is the one that dominates in this letter. Most of what is here in this letter is designed to provide tests of life: "I write these things…that you may know that you have eternal life." That is, that you may know you are born again.

Summing up all these reasons for writing 1 John goes like this: *I am writing because you are true believers, but there are deceivers in your midst, and I want you to be rock-solid confident in your present possession of eternal life as regenerate children of God, so that you are not drawn away after sin. And if this letter has that effect my joy will be complete.* So at the heart of his reason for writing is the desire to help them know they are born again—that they now have new spiritual life. Eternal life.

Eleven Evidences of the New Birth

Consider one more overview before we focus on 1 John 5:3–4. John gives at least eleven evidences that a person is born again. We could probably boil them all down to faith and love. But for now we'll let them stand the way he says them. Not every verse below uses new-birth language. But it will be plain, if you think about it for a moment, that even where the language is not present, the reality is. Here they are:

1. *Those who are born of God keep his commandments.*

> 1 John 2:3–4: "By this we know that we have come to know him, if we keep his commandments. Whoever says 'I know him' but does not keep his commandments is a liar, and the truth is not in him."

> 1 John 3:24: "Whoever keeps his commandments abides in God, and God in him."

2. *Those who are born of God walk as Christ walked.*

> 1 John 2:5–6: "By this we may know that we are in him: whoever says he abides in him ought to walk in the same way in which he walked."

3. *Those who are born of God don't hate others but love them.*

> 1 John 2:9: "Whoever says he is in the light and hates his brother is still in darkness."

> 1 John 3:14: "We know that we have passed out of death into life, because we love the brothers. Whoever does not love abides in death."

> 1 John 4:7–8: "Beloved, let us love one another, for love is from God, and whoever loves has been born of God and knows God. Anyone who does not love does not know God, because God is love."

> 1 John 4:20: "If anyone says, 'I love God,' and hates his brother, he is a liar."

4. *Those who are born of God don't love the world.*

> 1 John 2:15: "If anyone loves the world, the love of the Father is not in him."

5. *Those who are born of God confess the Son and receive (have) him.*

> 1 John 2:23: "No one who denies the Son has the Father. Whoever confesses the Son has the Father also."

> 1 John 4:15: "Whoever confesses that Jesus is the Son of God, God abides in him, and he in God."

> 1 John 5:12: "Whoever has the Son has life; whoever does not have the Son of God does not have life."

6. *Those who are born of God practice righteousness.*

> 1 John 2:29: "If you know that he is righteous, you may be sure that everyone who practices righteousness has been born of him."

7. *Those who are born of God don't make a practice of sinning.*

> 1 John 3:6: "No one who abides in him keeps on sinning; no one who keeps on sinning has either seen him or known him."

> 1 John 3:9–10: "No one born of God makes a practice of sinning, for God's seed abides in him, and he cannot keep on sinning because he has been born of God. By this it is evident who are the children of God, and who are the children of the devil: whoever does not practice righteousness is not of God, nor is the one who does not love his brother."

> 1 John 5:18: "We know that everyone who has been born of God does not keep on sinning, but he who was born of God protects him, and the evil one does not touch him."

8. *Those who are born of God possess the Spirit of God.*

> 1 John 3:24: "By this we know that he abides in us, by the Spirit whom he has given us."

1 John 4:13: "By this we know that we abide in him and he in us, because he has given us of his Spirit."

9. Those who are born of God listen submissively to the apostolic Word.

1 John 4:6: "We are from God. Whoever knows God listens to us; whoever is not from God does not listen to us. By this we know the Spirit of truth and the spirit of error."

10. Those who are born of God believe that Jesus is the Christ.

1 John 5:1: "Everyone who believes that Jesus is the Christ has been born of God."

11. Those who are born of God overcome the world.

1 John 5:4: "Everyone who has been born of God overcomes the world. And this is the victory that has overcome the world—our faith."

No Perfection, No Defection

One of the mistaken effects of all those "tests of life" would be to overwhelm us with the sense that John might possibly be saying: "If you're born again, you're perfect. If you're born again, you don't sin at all. There is no defeat in the Christian life. There is only victory." That would be a serious misreading of the letter.

Another mistaken effect that these tests might have on our minds is to make us think we can lose our salvation. They might make us think that we can be born again for a while and then begin to fail in these tests and die and lose the spiritual life that we were given in the new birth. That would be another serious mistake.

John is very aware that his words could be taken in these two wrong ways. So he is as explicit as any writer in the New

Testament that this is not the case: Christians are not sinless, and born-again people cannot lose the new birth and be lost.

He says in 1 John 1:8–10, "If we say we have no sin [present tense], we deceive ourselves, and the truth is not in us. If we confess our sins [present tense], he is faithful and just to forgive us our sins and to cleanse us from all unrighteousness. If we say we have not sinned, we make him a liar, and his word is not in us." So John is at pains to say that "walking in the light" (1:7) does not mean walking flawlessly. It means that, when you stumble, the light of Christ causes you to see your stumbling as sin and hate it and confess it and receive forgiveness and move forward with Christ.

And John is just as jealous to make sure we don't infer from these "tests of life" that we can be born again and then later lose our life and be lost. 1 John 2:19 is one of the clearest statements in the Bible that there is another way to understand what happens when a person abandons the church. It says, "They went out from us, but they were not of us; for if they had been of us, they would have continued with us. But they went out, that it might become plain that they all are not of us."

Notice three things John says to protect us from misunderstanding. 1) Those who seemed to be born again and forsook the faith never were born again—they never were of us. "They went out from us, but they were not of us." In other words, the explanation is not that they lost their new birth. They never had it. 2) Those who are truly born again (who are "of us") will persevere to the end in faith. Verse 19: "If they had been of us, they would have continued with us." Endurance is not the cause of the new birth. The new birth is the cause of endurance, and endurance is the evidence of new birth. 3) God often makes plain who the false Christians are in the church by their eventual rejection of the truth and the people of God. Verse 19: "They went out, that it might become plain that they all are not of us." It became plain. So today it often becomes plain who are "of us."

You recall that one of the tests of life in 1 John 4:6 was that those who truly know God listen to the apostolic teaching. They love it, and they cling to it. "Whoever knows God listens to us; whoever is not from God does not listen to us." These people listened for a while. The seed of the word sprang up, perhaps even with joy (Luke 8:13), and it looked as though they were truly born again. But then hard times came and the cares and riches and pleasures of life swept them away, and they showed that they had never been born again.

A Three-Link Chain in 1 John 5:3–4

Now briefly consider 1 John 5:3–4, and let it set the stage for a fuller treatment in the next chapter. Consider the way these thoughts fit together. Here's a three-link chain of thought: "[Link One] For this is the love of God, that we keep his commandments. And his commandments are not burdensome. [Link Two] For everyone who has been born of God overcomes the world. [Link Three] And this is the victory that has overcome the world—our faith."

Link One: Love for God is expressed in obedience to his commandments with a spirit that does not act burdensomely. Verse 3: "For this is the love of God, that we keep his commandments. And his commandments are not burdensome." The mark of love for God is willing, joyful obedience, not begrudging obedience.

Link Two: The basis of this unbegrudging obedience is the power of the new birth to overcome the world. Verse 4: "For [signifying the basis of what went before!] everyone who has been born of God overcomes the world." Our love for God obeys him freely and joyfully because in the new birth the spell of the world is broken and it loses its power. When the world loses its powerful attraction because of the new birth, God and his holy will become attractive. Not burdensome. How does this work?

Link Three: This world-defeating power that breaks the spell of sin and makes the will of God beautiful, not burdensome, is our faith. Verse 4: "And this is the victory that has overcome the world—our faith."

GOSPEL, NEW BIRTH, FAITH, AND OBEDIENCE WITH JOY

So the chain of thought goes like this: The new birth happens as we are brought into contact with the living and abiding word, the gospel. The first effect of this new birth is that we see and receive God and his Son and his work and his will as supremely beautiful and valuable. That's faith. This faith overcomes the world, that is, it overcomes the enslaving power of the world to be our supreme treasure.

Faith breaks the enslaving spell of the world's allurement. In that way, faith leads us into obedience with freedom and joy. God and his holy will look beautiful and not burdensome. The new birth has taken the blinders off. We see things for what they really are. We are free to obey with joy.

May God confirm your spiritual reality—your new birth— by overcoming the seductive power of the world in your life. "Everyone who has been born of God overcomes the world. And this is the victory that has overcome the world—our faith."

Everyone who believes that Jesus is the Christ has been born of God, and everyone who loves the Father loves whoever has been born of him. By this we know that we love the children of God, when we love God and obey his commandments. For this is the love of God, that we keep his commandments. And his commandments are not burdensome. For everyone who has been born of God overcomes the world. And this is the victory that has overcome the world—our faith. Who is it that overcomes the world except the one who believes that Jesus is the Son of God?

1 John 5:1–5

II

REGENERATION, FAITH, LOVE— IN THAT ORDER

In this chapter, we pick up on the very important text, 1 John 5:1–5, which we began to unpack in the last chapter. There is so much more. One of my aims here is to show that our ability to love others imperfectly is based on our assurance that in Christ we already love them perfectly. In other words, I want you to see for yourselves that, even when you fail to love as you ought, Christ's perfection stands before God in place of that failure. And I want you to see that faith in Christ, not love for people, is the way you enjoy that union with Christ. Therefore, faith must come first and be the root of love and be different from love. Otherwise, love will be destroyed.

If you don't come at love this way, your failures will probably overwhelm you with guilt and hopelessness. If that happens, you will give way either to hardworking legalism or fatalistic immorality.

Let's start where we left off at the end of the previous chapter, namely, with the chain of thought in 1 John 5:3–4. The reason we are starting here is to see how regeneration, faith in Christ, and love for people relate to each other. And what will make all the difference is whether you see it for yourselves in the word of God, not whether you read what I believe about it. That will guide how I lay it out.

The First Link: Loving Others

Verse 3 says, "This is the love of God, that we keep his commandments. And his commandments are not burdensome." Sometimes people equate keeping commandments with loving God. Often they quote John 14:15: "If you love me, you will keep my commandments." But this text clearly distinguishes loving Christ from obeying his commandments. If you love me—that's one thing—then you will keep my commandments—that's another thing. The one leads to the other. If you have the one, you will do the other. Love and commandment-keeping are not identical.

It's not wrong to say that loving Jesus, or loving God, includes doing what he commands. But that's not all it is. Which is why John says in 1 John 5:3, "And his commandments are not burdensome." Loving God is not just external obedience; it means having a heart for God that doesn't find his commandments burdensome.

And if the commandments are not burdensome, what are they? They are desirable. What you desire to do with your whole heart is not burdensome to do. Listen to the psalmist. Psalm 40:8: "I delight to do your will, O my God; your law is within my heart." Psalm 119:24: "Your testimonies are my delight; they are my counselors." Psalm 119:35: "Lead me in the path of your commandments, for I delight in it." Psalm 119:92: "If your law had not been my delight, I would have perished in my affliction." Loving God means admiring and valuing and treasuring and desiring him with such ardency and authenticity that his will is our delight and is not burdensome.

WHICH COMMANDMENTS?

Before we go to the next link in the chain of 1 John 5:3–4, let's be sure that we know what commandments of God the apostle John especially has in mind when he speaks about keeping the commandments of God as an expression of loving him. It's pretty obvious if we follow the train of thought from 4:20 forward. John says in 4:20, "If anyone says, 'I love God,' and hates his brother, he is a liar; for he who does not love his brother whom he has seen cannot love God whom he has not seen. And this commandment we have from him: whoever loves God must also love his brother." So it appears that the primary obedience that John has in mind which would show we love God is loving others, especially other believers.

He stays on this point in 1 John 5:1: "Everyone who loves the Father loves whoever has been born of him." So there it is again: The sign that you love God is that you love others, especially other believers. Then verse 2 turns it around and says that loving God is the sign that you love his children: "By this we know that we love the children of God, when we love God and obey his commandments." I think the point of this is to guard against sentimental reinterpretations of what love is—reinterpretations that leave God and his commandments totally out of account. John is saying: Don't do that. You don't love anybody if you don't love God. You may think you do. But John says in verse 2, "By this we know that we love the children of God, when we love God."

If you don't love God, you can't do anybody any ultimate good. You can feed them and clothe them and house them and keep them comfortable while they perish. But in God's mind, that by itself is not what love is. Love does feed and clothe and house—and keeps the commandments that include helping others know and love God in Christ. But if you don't love God, you can't do that. So if you don't love God, you can't love people in the way that counts for eternity.

So we have our answer: When John says, "This is the love of God, that we keep his commandments. And his commandments are not burdensome," he mainly means the commandments summed up in loving other people, especially believers, and loving them in a way that counts forever. So we could paraphrase verse 3 like this: "This is the love of God, that we love others, especially his children, and that this life of sacrificial Christ-like love is not burdensome. It's what we most deeply desire to do as an expression of our love for the Father."

THE SECOND LINK: THE NEW BIRTH

Now the second link in the chain of thought in 1 John 5:3–4 is the first part of verse 4: "For everyone who has been born of God overcomes the world." Notice the word *for* at the beginning. John says that he is now going to explain *why* loving God by doing his commandments—that is, by loving other people—is not burdensome. It's not burdensome, he says in verse 4, "because everyone who has been born of God overcomes the world." How is that an argument?

We are able to love God and love others because in the new birth we have conquered the world. "Everyone who has been born of God conquers the world." This must mean that there are forces in the world that work to make us not love God and not love each other. And in the new birth these forces have been overcome.

What would those forces be? Let's go to 1 John 2:15–17 for the clearest answer in this letter:

> Do not love the world or the things in the world. If anyone loves the world, the love of the Father is not in him. For all that is in the world—the desires of the flesh and the desires of the eyes and pride in possessions—is not from the Father but is from the world. And the world is passing away along with its desires, but whoever does the will of God abides forever.

Here are the forces in the world that have to be overcome (v. 16): "the desires of the flesh and the desires of the eyes and pride in possessions." That could be summed up as desires for what we don't have, and pride in what we do have. When we *don't* have what we want, the world corrupts us with covetousness. And when we *do* have what we want the world corrupts us with pride.

This is what keeps us from loving God and loving each other. We love stuff. And when we don't have it, we crave it. And when we do have it, we love to talk about it incessantly, and waste time on it. And where is God in all that? At best, he's there as the cosmic Sugar Daddy. We may even thank him for all our stuff. But there is a kind of gratitude that proves that the gift, and not the Giver, is our god.

The main reason we don't love God and find it burdensome to love people is that our cravings are for the things of the world. They may be good things. They may be bad things. They may be material things. They may be relational. Whatever their form, they are not God. And when we crave them above God, they are idols. They replace love for God and love for people. That's the universal problem of the world. What's the solution?

John's answer is in 1 John 5:3–4. He says that the reason loving God and loving people is not burdensome (v. 3) is that we have been born again, and this new birth conquers the world: "Everyone who has been born of God overcomes the world." Now we can see what that means. It means that the new birth severs the root of those cravings for the world. Overcoming the world means that the desires of the flesh and the desires of the eyes and the pride in possessions don't rule us anymore. Their power is broken.

THE THIRD LINK: FAITH IN JESUS

How does that work? That's what the last half of verse 4 tells us (the third link in the chain): "And this is the victory that has overcome the world—our faith." The reason the new birth conquers the desires of the flesh and the desires of the eyes and the pride in possessions is that it creates faith.

The most immediate and decisive work of God in the new birth is that the new life he creates sees the superior value of Jesus over all else (2 Cor. 4:4, 6). And with no lapse of time at all, this spiritual sight of the superior value of Jesus results in receiving Jesus as the Treasure that he is. That is faith: receiving Jesus for all that he is because our eyes have been opened to see his truth and beauty and worth.

That is why faith conquers the world. The world held us in bondage by the power of its desires. But now our eyes have been opened by the new birth to see the superior desirability of Jesus. Jesus is better than the desires of the flesh, and better than the desires of the eyes, and better than the riches that strangle us with greed and pride (Mark 4:19).

THE ORDER: NEW BIRTH, FAITH, LOVE

Now we are in a position to answer our original question about the relationship between regeneration, faith in Christ, and loving people. Here's what we can say and why it's so important.

We can say, first, that regeneration is the cause of faith. That's plain in 1 John 5:1: "Everyone who believes [that is, has faith] that Jesus is the Christ has been born of God." Having been born of

could it be?

regeneration > faith > loving.

begetting > belonging > (fruit) bearing

born again. > believing >

God results in our believing. Our believing is the immediate evidence of God's begetting.

Second, we can say that loving people is the fruit of this faith. That's the way John argues in verse 4: The victory that overcomes the world—that is, that overcomes the obstacles to loving others—is our faith.

So in the order of causation, we have: 1) new birth, 2) faith in Jesus, and 3) the doing of God's commandments without a sense of burdensomeness, namely, loving others. God causes the new birth. The new birth is the creation of new life that sees Christ for who he is and receives him; and that receiving severs the roots of the cravings of the world and sets us free to love.

Now why is this order so important?

It's important because it will keep us from confusing saving faith and love for people. There are some today who are combining faith in Christ and love for people. They are saying that faith really means faithfulness and that faithfulness includes love for people, and so there is no way to distinguish faith in Christ and love for people.

FAITH AND LOVE: INSEPARABLE BUT DISTINGUISHABLE

But conflating faith in Christ and love for people is a deadly mistake. I'll try to say why. Faith in Christ and love for people *are* inseparable. But they are not indistinguishable. They are so inseparable that John can sum up all God's demands in these two: faith and love. 1 John 3:23: "This is his commandment [singular], that we *believe* in the name of his Son Jesus Christ and *love* one another, just as he has commanded us." That is the summary of all the tests of life in John's letter: Believe on Jesus and love each other.

But the order of causality is crucial. The reason it's crucial is this: There is going to come a day when you do not love as you ought. What will you do if your heart condemns you because you know that love is a sign of the new birth? How will you fight the fight for assurance at that time?

JESUS THE RIGHTEOUS

Here is one crucial way to fight for your hope at that moment, and it depends on a clear distinction between faith in Christ and love for people: Go to 1 John 2:1 and read, "My little children, I am writing these things to you so that you may not sin. But if anyone does sin [that is, fails to love others as he ought], we have an advocate with the Father, Jesus Christ the righteous." John assumes that even when you fail—even when you sin, when you do not love as you ought—you have an advocate before God. And this advocate is called "the righteous one." That is, he is perfect. (See Rom. 8:33–34.)

Even if you have sinned, he has never sinned. Even if you have failed to love as you ought, he has never failed to love as he ought. And this perfect one stands before God and advocates for you—not against you, but for you. Precisely because you have failed. "But if anyone does sin, we have an advocate...the righteous one."

The emphasis falls on his righteousness—his sinlessness. His perfectly doing what we have failed to do. The reason this works for us is that faith is what receives him. And when faith receives him, he is everything that we need before God. He is our righteousness and our perfection and our perfect love. This is the bottom of our hope before a holy God.

This is why it is so crucial to see that believing in Jesus is different from loving people and is the root of it. Believing in Jesus means receiving him. Loving others means going out to them. We are able to go out to them imperfectly because we have received Jesus as our perfection. Receiving Jesus means that he is the ground of our salvation. He is the bottom of the foundation of our hope. It is his righteousness and his perfection and his love ultimately that counts for us before the Father. Faith in Jesus, not love for people, receives Jesus as my substitute righteousness and perfection and love.

That is why I can have hope even when I stumble. My standing with God does not go up and down, or in and out, with my walking and stumbling. My standing with God is the righteousness of my Advocate. My perfect Advocate, Jesus Christ, says today, "Father, for my sake, look with favor on your imperfect servant John. For the sake of my perfect love, look with favor on him in his imperfect love. You know all things, Father (1 John 3:20). You know that in his heart he is banking on me and trusts me. Therefore, I am his, and my perfect love counts as his."

OUR PERFECT ADVOCATE

God sees me in Christ. And I don't despair because of my failure. I am not paralyzed with hopelessness. I confess my failure to love (1 John 1:9). I embrace the forgiveness he bought. I take my stand on the wrath-removing propitiation he provided (1 John 2:2). And I reassure my heart (1 John 3:19) that God sees me through my Advocate—my perfect Advocate.

So I end where I started. I wanted you to see for yourselves that our ability to love others imperfectly is based on the fact that in Christ we already love them perfectly. That is, his loving them perfectly counts as our loving them perfectly if we are in him by faith alone. He is the perfection that we need before God. And we have it not by loving others, but by trusting him. This very assurance is the key to loving others. And if we lose this key, we lose everything, including the power to love others.

See what kind of love the Father has given to us, that we should be called children of God; and so we are. The reason why the world does not know us is that it did not know him. Beloved, we are God's children now, and what we will be has not yet appeared; but we know that when he appears we shall be like him, because we shall see him as he is. And everyone who thus hopes in him purifies himself as he is pure. Everyone who makes a practice of sinning also practices lawlessness; sin is lawlessness. You know that he appeared to take away sins, and in him there is no sin. No one who abides in him keeps on sinning; no one who keeps on sinning has either seen him or known him. Little children, let no one deceive you. Whoever practices righteousness is righteous, as he is righteous. Whoever makes a practice of sinning is of the devil, for the devil has been sinning from the beginning. The reason the Son of God appeared was to destroy the works of the devil. No one born of God makes a practice of sinning, for God's seed abides in him, and he cannot keep on sinning because he has been born of God. By this it is evident who are the children of God, and who are the children of the devil: whoever does not practice righteousness is not of God, nor is the one who does not love his brother.

1 John 3:1–10

12

FREEDOM FROM
THE PRACTICE OF SINNING

The question we will tackle in this chapter is: *How do people who
have experienced the miracle of the new birth deal with their own
sinfulness as they try to live in the full assurance of their salvation?*
That is, how do we deal with the conflict between the reality
of the new birth, on the one hand, and our ongoing sin, on the
other hand? How do we balance the danger of losing assurance
of salvation and the danger of being presumptuous that we are
born again when we may not be? How can we enjoy the assurance
of being born again, and yet not take lightly the sinfulness of
our lives that is so out of step with being born again?

GOD CALLS US TO FULL ASSURANCE

The First Epistle of John, more than any other book in the Bible,
seems to be designed to help us in this practical, daily battle.
Consider 1 John 5:13: "I write these things to you who believe in
the name of the Son of God that you may know that you have

eternal life." This book is written, he says, to help believers have the full assurance that they have been born again—that is, that they have new, spiritual life in them that will never die. John wants us—God wants us—to experience something through this letter that makes us profoundly confident that we have passed from death to life.

1 John 3:14 says, "We know that we have passed out of death into life." Jesus says in John 5:24, "Truly, truly, I say to you, whoever hears my word and believes him who sent me has eternal life. He does not come into judgment, but has passed from death to life." So John and Jesus are jealous for us believers to know that judgment and death are behind us because our judgment happened when Jesus was judged in our place, and our death happened when Jesus died in our place. And therefore, new life is in us, and this life cannot perish and cannot be taken away. It's eternal. That's the assurance John and Jesus want for us. "I write these things to you...that you may know that you have eternal life" (1 John 5:13).

What the False Teachers Said

But something is going on in the churches that John is writing to that concerns him deeply. Whatever it is, it threatens to destroy this assurance. There are false teachers who are saying things that may give the impression of good news and strong assurance, but will have the very opposite effect. In dealing with these false teachers, John shows us how to deal with our own sin in relation to our struggle for assurance. What were these false teachers saying?

First, they were saying that the preexistent Son of God, Jesus Christ, had not come in the flesh. They did not believe in the full union of the preexistent Son of God with a fleshly human nature like ours. Here is what John says about them in 1 John 4:1–3:

Beloved, do not believe every spirit, but test the spirits to see whether they are from God, for many false prophets have gone out into the world. By this you know the Spirit of God: every spirit that confesses that Jesus Christ has come in the flesh is from God, and every spirit that does not confess Jesus is not from God.

These false teachers disconnected Christ and the flesh. We see that in verse 2. John insisted on the very thing some were denying: "Every spirit that confesses that *Jesus Christ has come in the flesh* is from God." They did not like the idea of the preexistent Christ being united with human flesh.

BAD CHRISTOLOGY YIELDS BAD MORALITY

Here is the reason that's relevant for our question in this chapter. This view of the person of Christ not being united to physical flesh evidently had a practical, moral effect on the way these false teachers viewed the Christian life. Just as they disconnected the person of Christ from ordinary physical life, so they disconnected being a Christian from ordinary physical life.

One of the clearest places to see this is here in our text: 1 John 3:7. John says, "Little children, let no one deceive you [so he has the false teachers in view]. Whoever practices righteousness is righteous, as he is righteous." What's he saying? He is saying. "Beware of the false teachers because what they say is that you can be righteous and not practice righteousness." "Let no one deceive you. Whoever practices righteousness is righteous."

In other words, John opposes not only their view of Christ, that they disconnect his person from his ordinary bodily life of doing things, but he also opposes their view of the Christian life when they disconnect our person from our ordinary bodily life of doing things. "The flesh didn't really matter for Jesus," the false teachers say. "What matters is that somehow, in a spiritual way, he is the Christ, and there is no real union of the preexistent Christ and the physical man Jesus. And our flesh doesn't really matter either; but somehow, in a spiritual way, we are born again, but there is no real union between that new creation and our physical life that does righteousness or does sin." Which led directly to the error that John points out in 1 John 3:7—that you can be righteous in some spiritual way, and yet not do righteousness in your ordinary physical life.

John has three responses to this false teaching.

CHRIST'S INCARNATION LASTS FOREVER

First, he insists that the flesh of Jesus and the person of the pre-existent Christ are inseparable after the incarnation. 1 John 4:2: "By this you know the Spirit of God: every spirit that confesses that Jesus Christ has come in the flesh is from God." Notice it does not say *"came* in the flesh," as though that union with flesh and bones happened for a while and then stopped. He says, *"has come* in the flesh."

This incarnation lasts forever. The second person of the Trinity will forever be united with human nature. We will always know him as Jesus, one like us, and infinitely above us—the firstborn among many brothers (Rom. 8:29). God did not, and does not, despise the physical creation that he made. He has come in the flesh. And the Son of God remains in the flesh forever. So John's first response to the false teaching is to set straight their view of Christ. His physical being is not a mirage. It's not secondary. It's not unimportant. That he has a body marks and identifies him forever.

CHRISTIAN DOING CONFIRMS BEING

John's second response to the false teaching is to deny emphatically its teaching that spiritual *being* can be separated from physical *doing*. John, in fact, insists that spiritual being must be validated by physical doing, or else the spiritual being is simply not real. That's what we saw in 1 John 3:7: "Little children, let no one deceive you. Whoever *practices* righteousness *is* righteous, as he is righteous." The deceivers were saying: You can *be* righteous and yet not *practice* righteousness. John says: The only people who *are* righteous are the ones who *practice* righteousness. Doing confirms being.

That is what John says over and over again in this letter. For example, in 1 John 2:29, he says, "If you know that he is righteous, you may be sure that everyone who practices righteousness has been born of him." In other words, the doing of righteousness is the evidence and confirmation of being born again.

Or consider 1 John 3:9: "No one born of God makes a practice of sinning, for God's seed abides in him, and he cannot keep on sinning because he has been born of God." The practice of sin is the evidence and confirmation that one is not born of God. Doing confirms being. Not practicing sin is the evidence and confirmation of being born again.

And the reason the new birth inevitably changes the life of sinning, John says, is that when we are born again, "God's seed" abides in us, and we "cannot keep on sinning." That's how real the connection between the new birth and daily physical life is. The "seed" here may be the Spirit of God or the word of God or the nature of God—or all three. Whatever it is specifically, God himself is at work in the new birth so powerfully that we cannot keep on practicing sin. God's new presence cannot make peace with a pattern of sinful behavior.

These false teachers who think they can separate who they are spiritually from who they are physically do not understand either the incarnation or regeneration. In the incarnation, the preexistent Christ is really united with a physical body. And in regeneration, the new creation in Christ has real, inevitable effects on our physical life of obedience.

The Regenerate Are Not Sinless

John's third response to the false teaching is to reject any notion of sinlessness in born-again people. Evidently, the way this false teaching was working was that, by disconnecting *"being* righteous" from *"doing* righteousness" (3:7), they were then able to say, "Well, even if your body does some things that are sinful, that's not really you. The real you is the born-again you; and that real you is so above daily physical life that it's never defiled by sin."

So this disconnection that the false teachers made between who you are and what you do had led them, evidently, to say that Christians never really sin. How could we sin? We're born of God. We're new creatures. We have the seed of God in us. So John levels his guns at this error three times. It's important that you see them in the text for yourself, because they are meant for your personal use in defeating the accusations of Satan that your sins prove you are not born again.

First, 1 John 1:8: "If we say we have no sin, we deceive ourselves, and the truth is not in us." We! We born-again Christians. In other words, don't let the deception of these false teachers work its way into your own self-deception. There are no sinless Christians.

Second, 1 John 2:1: "My little children, I am writing these things to you so that you may not sin. But if anyone does sin, we have an advocate with the Father, Jesus Christ the righteous." In other words, John does not assume that if you sin, you are not born again. He assumes that if you sin, you have an Advocate. And only those who are born again have this Advocate.

Third, 1 John 5:16-17: "If anyone sees his brother committing a sin not leading to death, he shall ask, and God will give him life—to those who commit sins that do not lead to death. There is sin that leads to death; I do not say that one should pray for that. All wrongdoing is sin, but there is sin that does not lead to death."

Notice that last clause: "There is sin that does not lead to death." This is why you can see your brother committing sin. He is your brother. He is born again. And he is sinning. How can this be? Because there is sin that does not lead to death. I don't think John has particular kinds of sins in view, but rather degrees of rootedness and habitual persistence. There is a point of confirmed sinning which may take you over the line of no return and you will be like Esau who sought repentance with tears and could not find it (Heb. 12:16–17). He could not repent. If he could have, there would have been forgiveness. But the heart can become so hardened by sin that even its desires to repent are counterfeit.

DEALING WITH OUR ONGOING SIN

Now we come to the question we raised at the beginning: How do people who have experienced the miracle of the new birth deal with their own sinfulness as they try to live in the full assurance of their salvation? My answer is: You deal with it by the way you use John's teaching. John warns against hypocrisy (claiming to be born again when your life contradicts it), and John celebrates the Advocacy and Propitiation of Christ for born-again sinners.

The question is: How do you use these two truths? How do you use the warning that you might deceive yourself? How do you use the promise, "If we do sin, we have an Advocate"? The evidence of your new birth lies in how these two truths function in your life.

Here's the way they function if you are born again:

FLEEING PRESUMPTION, FLYING TO THE ADVOCATE

One common scenario for believers is drifting toward sinful presumption. You are slipping into a lukewarm, careless, presumptuous frame of mind about your own sinfulness. You are starting to coast or be indifferent to whether you are holy or worldly. You are losing your vigilance against bad attitudes and behaviors— and starting to settle in with sinful patterns of behavior.

When the born-again person experiences this kind of drift, the truth of 1 John 3:9 ("No one born of God makes a practice of sinning") has the effect, by the Holy Spirit, of awakening him to the danger of his condition so that he flies to his Advocate and his Propitiation for mercy and forgiveness and righteousness. He confesses his sin and receives cleansing (1:9). His love for Christ is renewed and the sweetness of his relationship is recovered and the hatred of sin is restored and the joy of the Lord again becomes his strength.

FLEEING DESPAIR, FLYING TO THE ADVOCATE

Another common scenario for believers is drifting toward despair. You are sinking down in fear and discouragement and even despair that your righteousness, your love for people, and your fight against sin are just not good enough. Your conscience is condemning you, and your own deeds seem so imperfect to you that they could never prove that you are born again.

When the born-again person experiences this, the truth of 1 John 2:1 has the effect, by the Spirit, of rescuing him from despair: "My little children [he wants to be tender with our consciences], I am writing these things to you so that you may not sin. But if anyone does sin, we have an advocate with the Father, Jesus Christ the righteous."

John's warning of hypocrisy calls us back from the precipice of presumption. John's promise of an Advocate calls us back from the precipice of despair.

THE REDEMPTIVE POWER OF GOD'S WORD

The new birth enables you to hear Scripture and use Scripture helpfully, redemptively. The new birth doesn't use the promise "We have an Advocate" to justify an attitude of cavalier indifference to sin. The new birth doesn't use the warning "No one born of God makes a practice of sinning" to pour gasoline on the fires of despair. The new birth brings a spiritual discernment that senses how to use John's teaching: The new birth is chastened and sobered by the warnings, and the new birth is thrilled and empowered by the promise of an Advocate and a Propitiation.

May the Lord confirm your new birth as you experience both of these responses to the word of God. May he grant you to embrace both the warning and the comfort. May you hear the word of God as God means it to be heard, and may God's all-sufficient word preserve the full assurance of your salvation.

*Beloved, let us love one another, for love is from God,
and whoever loves has been born of God and knows God.
Anyone who does not love does not know God, because
God is love. In this the love of God was made manifest
among us, that God sent his only Son into the world,
so that we might live through him. In this is love, not
that we have loved God but that he loved us and sent
his Son to be the propitiation for our sins. Beloved, if
God so loved us, we also ought to love one another. No
one has ever seen God; if we love one another, God
abides in us and his love is perfected in us. By this we
know that we abide in him and he in us, because he
has given us of his Spirit. And we have seen and testify
that the Father has sent his Son to be the Savior of the
world. Whoever confesses that Jesus is the Son of God,
God abides in him, and he in God. So we have come to
know and to believe the love that God has for us. God
is love, and whoever abides in love abides in God, and
God abides in him. By this is love perfected with us, so
that we may have confidence for the day of judgment,
because as he is so also are we in this world. There is
no fear in love, but perfect love casts out fear. For fear
has to do with punishment, and whoever fears has not
been perfected in love. We love because he first loved us.
If anyone says, "I love God," and hates his brother, he
is a liar; for he who does not love his brother whom he
has seen cannot love God whom he has not seen. And
this commandment we have from him: whoever loves
God must also love his brother.*

1 John 4:7–21

13

LOVING OTHERS WITH THE LOVE OF GOD

The aspect of the new birth we will focus on in this chapter is the fact that the new birth creates the connection between God's love for us and our love for each other. If anyone ever asks, *How does the fact that God loves you result in your loving others?* the answer is: The new birth creates that connection. The new birth is the act of the Holy Spirit connecting our dead, selfish hearts with God's living, loving heart so that his life becomes our life and his love becomes our love.

This is clearly seen in 1 John 4:7–12. John shows the link in two ways: First, he shows that God's nature is love, so that when we are born again by him we share that nature; and second, he shows that the manifestation of that nature in history was the sending of his Son so that we might have eternal life through him. Let's take these one at a time and notice how they are connected to the new birth.

GOD'S NATURE IS LOVE

First, verses 7–8: God's nature is love. "Beloved, let us love one another, for love is from God, and whoever loves has been born of God and knows God. Anyone who does not love does not know God, because God is love." Notice it says two things. Verse 7 says that "love *is from* God." And verse 8 at the end says, "God *is* love." These are not at odds, because when John says that "love is *from* God," he doesn't mean it's from him the way letters are from a mailman, or even from a friend. He means that love is from God the way heat is from fire, or the way light is from the sun. Love belongs to God's nature. It's woven into what he is. It's part of what it means to be God. The sun gives light because it is light. And fire gives heat because it is heat.

So John's point is that in the new birth, this aspect of the divine nature becomes part of who you are. The new birth is the imparting to you of divine life, and an indispensable part of that life is love. God's nature is love, and in the new birth that nature becomes part of who you are.

Notice verse 12: "No one has ever seen God; if we love one another, God abides in us and his love is perfected in us." When you are born again, God himself is imparted to you. He dwells in you and sheds abroad in your heart his love (Rom. 5:5). And his aim is that this love be perfected in you. Notice the phrase "his love" in verse 12. The love that you have as a born-again person is no mere imitation of the divine love. It is an experience of the divine love and an extension of that love to others.

So the first way John links God's love for us and our love for people is by focusing on God's nature as love and how the new birth connects us to that.

GOD'S LOVE REVEALED IN SENDING HIS SON

Then, second, consider 1 John 4:9–11, where John focuses on the main *manifestation* of that divine love in history.

> In this the love of God was made manifest among us, that God sent his only Son into the world, so that we might live

through him. In this is love, not that we have loved God but that he loved us and sent his Son to be the propitiation for our sins. Beloved, if God so loved us, we also ought to love one another.

In John's mind, the great manifestation of God's love is that God sent his Son—John says this twice in verses 9–10. The aim of that sending, he says, was to be the propitiation for our sins. That's what makes the sending to be love. And what is propitiation? It means that he came to bear the punishment for sin and thus be the one who removes the wrath of God from us (Rom. 8:3; Gal. 3:13).

Think of it! This means that it was God's love that sent his Son to bear God's just penalty and to take away God's just wrath. The greatest manifestation of the love of God is God's unilateral action to satisfy his own wrath.

And the way the Son does this is mentioned in 1 John 3:16: "By this we know love, that he laid down his life for us." So the Son became our propitiation by laying down his life for us. Dying for us. And John says this is the manifestation of God's nature. This is the way God is.

Notice another note that John strikes in verse 10: "In this is love, not that we have loved God but that he loved us and sent his Son." What is he guarding against in that denial: "In this is love, not that we have loved God…"? He is emphasizing that the nature and the origin of love does not lie in our response to God. That is not where love starts. That is not mainly what love is. Love starts with God. And if anything we feel or do can be called love, it will be because we are connected with God by the new birth.

Now we have seen two things about God's love. First, John shows that God's nature is love, so that when we are born again by him, we share that nature; and second, he shows that the manifestation of that love in history was the sending of his Son so that we might have eternal life through him.

WHAT DOES OUGHT MEAN?

Now don't miss the crucial place of the new birth in relation to the manifestation of God's love as well as the nature of God's love. John says in 1 John 4:11, "Beloved, if God so loved us [that is, sent his Son in this way for us], we also *ought* to love one another." When John writes that, how are we to understand this word *ought*? If you forgot everything in the preceding five verses, you might be able to say: "Well, the point of the incarnation is imitation. God loved us. We look at how he did it and we do it too. We're obliged to imitate him."

But John has not forgotten what he wrote in verses 7–8. "Whoever loves has been born of God and knows God. Anyone who does not love does not know God, because God is love." So when he says, "We ought to love each other," he means ought in the way that fish ought to swim in water and birds ought to fly in the air and living creatures ought to breathe and peaches ought to be sweet and lemons ought to be sour and hyenas ought to laugh. And born-again people ought to love. It's who we are.

This is not mere imitation. For the children of God, imitation becomes realization. We are realizing and expressing who we are when we love. God's seed is in us. God's Spirit is in us. God's nature is in us. God's love is being perfected in us.

Yes, there is the external impulse of seeing in history the Son of God laying down his life for us and constraining us in this way. But what's unique about the Christian life is that there is also the internal impulse that comes from being born again and having the very love that sent the Son into the world pulsing through our souls by the life of God within. The new birth enables us to experience the manifestation of God's love in history as an internal reality of God's Spirit within us.

So I return to what I said at the beginning of the chapter. The aspect of the new birth that I want us to focus on is the fact that the new birth creates the connection between God's love for us and our love for each other. If anyone ever asks, "How does the fact that God loves you result in your loving others?" the answer is: The new birth creates that connection. The new birth is the act of the Holy Spirit connecting our dead, selfish hearts with God's living, loving heart so that his life becomes our life and his love becomes our love.

We have seen that this love is both by nature who God is, and by manifestation what God has done in history sending, his own Son to lay down his life that he might be the propitiation for our sins and that we might have eternal life. The new birth connects us to this manifestation of love in such a way that it defines who we are as the children of God. If we are born again, we love each other.

HOW THE BORN AGAIN LOVE

What I want to do for the rest of this chapter is apply what we have seen to how we practically love each other. "Beloved, if God so loved us, we also ought to love one another." If we are regenerate people, we are loving people. If we are born again, the love of God is within us. "We know that we have passed out of death into life, because we love the brothers" (1 John 3:14).

What will this look like?

John mentions several specific ways that the love of God will become real in our lives through the new birth. I'll mention two.

HUMBLY REJOICING IN THE GOODNESS OF OTHERS

> This is the message that you have heard from the beginning, that we should love one another. We should not be like Cain, who was of the evil one and murdered his brother. And why did he murder him? Because his own deeds were evil and his brother's righteous. Do not be surprised, brothers, that the world hates you. We know that we have passed out of death into life, because we love the brothers. (1 John 3:11–14)

Now this specific form of love in verse 12 may seem to you to be totally unneeded. "Don't be like Cain who murdered his brother." Am I really concerned that there will be a spate of murders among Christians? No. And I don't think John feared that either, though it does happen. He doesn't focus on the murder. He asks in verse 12, "And why did he murder him?" That's John's concern. There is something about Cain's motive that he thinks will be relevant to the way believers love each other.

He answers at the end of verse 12: "Because his own deeds were evil and his brother's righteous." What John is saying here is not merely that love doesn't kill a brother, but that love doesn't feel resentful when a brother is superior in some spiritual or moral way. Cain didn't kill Abel simply because Cain was evil. He killed him because the contrast between Abel's goodness and Cain's evil made Cain angry. It made him feel guilty. Abel didn't have to say anything; Abel's goodness was a constant reminder to Cain that he was evil. And instead of dealing with his own evil by repentance and change, he got rid of Abel. If you don't like what you see in the mirror, shoot the mirror.

So what would it be like for any of us to be like Cain? It would mean that anytime some weakness or bad habit in our lives is exposed by contrast to someone else's goodness, instead of dealing with the weakness or the bad habit, we keep away from those whose lives make us feel defective. We don't kill them. We avoid them. Or worse, we find ways to criticize them so as to neutralize the part of their lives that was making us feel convicted. We feel like the best way to nullify someone's good point is to draw attention to his bad point. And so we protect ourselves from whatever good he might be for us.

But John's point is: Love doesn't act like that. Love is glad when our brothers and sisters are making progress in good habits or good attitudes or good behavior. Love rejoices in this growth. And if it happens to be faster than our own growth, then love is humble and rejoices with those who rejoice.

So the lesson for us is: Everywhere you see some growth, some virtue, some spiritual discipline, some good habit, or good attitude, rejoice in it. Give thanks for it. Compliment it. Don't resent it. Don't be like Cain. Respond the opposite from Cain. Be inspired by other people's goodness.

Love is humble. Love delights in other people's good. Love doesn't protect its own flaws. Love takes steps to change them. What a beautiful fellowship where everyone is rejoicing in each other's strengths, not resenting them! This is what the love of God looks like when the new birth gives it life in the people of God.

MEETING THE NEEDS OF OTHERS—EVEN AT GREAT COST

The second specific way John says the love of God becomes real in our lives through the new birth is found in 1 John 3:16–18:

> By this we know love, that he laid down his life for us, and we ought to lay down our lives for the brothers. But if anyone has the world's goods and sees his brother in need, yet closes his heart against him, how does God's love abide in him? Little children, let us not love in word or talk but in deed and in truth.

He says three things about love here, and they are increasingly specific. First, he says that love does practical things for people. Verse 18: "Little children, let us not love in word or talk but in deed and in truth." He doesn't mean that talk is not an important way of loving people. The tongue is full of potential for love and hate. What he does mean is that where deeds of practical help are called for, don't settle for talk. Do practical things for each other.

Then he tells us something about how seriously we should take this. Verse 16: "We ought to lay down our lives for the brothers." Christ loved us by laying down his life for us. When we were born again, this love became our love. There is in the born-again person a deep impulse to die to self that others might live. The presence of Christ in the born-again person is the presence of a servant's heart. A sacrificial spirit. A readiness to go down that others might go up. Love does not want to prosper at the expense of others. Love wants others to prosper, and if it costs us our life, that's okay. Jesus will take care of us.

So the first thing John says is that love is practical and does good for others. And the second thing he says is that we will do this even if it is very costly. "He laid down his life for us, and we ought to lay down our lives for the brothers."

Third, he says that this will mean very practical sacrifices in order to give people the things they need. Verse 17: "If anyone has the world's goods and sees his brother in need, yet closes his heart against him, how does God's love abide in him?" The main way John has in mind for us to lay down our lives for each other is that we share what we have. Love doesn't think possessively. Love knows that everything belongs to God. We are only managers of his possessions. Everything we have is at his disposal. And God is love. And when we were born again, his love became our love. And now his love governs his possessions in our hands.

So let's first be a very practical people who love in deeds and not just words. Then let's be a sacrificial people who deny ourselves for the sake of others and lay down our lives the way Christ laid down his life. And then let's be a lavishly generous people with everything we have, knowing that it all belongs to God, and we belong to God. We are his children. We have his nature. And he is love.

May the Lord grant us to focus in a fresh way on the love God manifest in sending his Son, and in his Son laying down his life to show us what the Father's love is like. And as we focus on the glories of the love of God in Christ, let's pray earnestly that the new birth would be confirmed among us as it creates the connection between God's love for us and our love for each other.

Beloved, let us love one another,
for love is from God,
and whoever loves has been born of God
and knows God.

1 John 4:7

Part Five

How Can We Help Others Be Born Again?

Having purified your souls by your obedience to the truth for a sincere brotherly love, love one another earnestly from a pure heart, since you have been born again, not of perishable seed but of imperishable, through the living and abiding word of God; for "All flesh is like grass and all its glory like the flower of grass. The grass withers, and the flower falls, but the word of the Lord remains forever." And this word is the good news that was preached to you. So put away all malice and all deceit and hypocrisy and envy and all slander. Like newborn infants, long for the pure spiritual milk, that by it you may grow up to salvation—if indeed you have tasted that the Lord is good.

1 Peter 1:22–2:3

14

TELL PEOPLE
THE GOOD NEWS OF JESUS CHRIST

The biblical truth that saving faith is possible only because God causes unbelievers to be born again (1 John 5:1) may make us feel empowered and encouraged and bold and hopeful in our personal evangelism, or it may make us feel fatalistic, pointless, unmotivated, and paralyzed in our evangelism. If we feel fatalistic and pointless and unmotivated and paralyzed in our witness to unbelievers, our feelings are out of sync with the truth, and we should ask the Lord to change our feelings.

This is the way I live my life every day—seeking to bring my vagrant feelings into line with ultimate reality. My feelings are not God. God is God. My feelings do not define truth. God's word defines truth. My feelings are echoes and responses to what my mind perceives. And sometimes—many times—my feelings are out of sync with the truth. When that happens—and it happens every day in some measure—I try not to bend the truth to justify my imperfect feelings, but rather, I plead with

God: Purify my perceptions of your truth and transform my feelings so that they are in sync with the truth.

That's the way I live my life every day. I hope you are with me in that battle.

So if I find myself feeling discouraged or pointless or unmotivated or paralyzed in my witness to unbelievers because of some biblical truth—like the fact that God's work in the new birth precedes and enables saving faith—then I lift my heart to the Lord and say, "O God, this truth is manifest in your word; grant that, by your Spirit, I would see this truth in a way that sets me free, and empowers me, and encourages me, and makes me joyful and bold in my witness, and hopeful in my evangelism."

I pray that you will grow, as I am trying to grow, in the wisdom of how to avail yourself of the power of the Holy Spirit to put to death feelings that are out of sync with the truth, and how to lay hold on God for the transformation of your feelings so that they match the truth of God's word.

GOOD NEWS, HEART OF LOVE, LIFE OF SERVICE

All that is preface to these final two chapters with their focus on evangelism. I am burdened to answer the question of what our role is in helping people to be born again. Implied in what we have seen in this book so far is the truth that God's role in bringing about the new birth is *decisive*, and our role in bringing about the new birth is *essential*. If these things are so, what should we be doing to help unbelievers to be born again?

The biblical answer is not obscure, and it's not complicated. The answer is: Tell people the good news of Christ from a heart of love and a life of service. You get a little picture of that combination in 2 Corinthians 4:5: "What we proclaim is not ourselves, but Jesus Christ as Lord, with ourselves as your servants for

Jesus' sake." Proclaiming Christ as Lord and offering ourselves as servants.

Haughty, condescending proclamation of Christ, with no feeling of brokenness or servanthood, contradicts the gospel. And silent servanthood that never speaks the gospel contradicts love. "We proclaim Jesus Christ as Lord with ourselves as your servants." That's what we do to help people to be born again. We tell people the good news of Christ from a heart of love and a life of service.

THE MOST IMPORTANT VERSE

We go again to 1 Peter 1:22–25 to see the connection between the new birth and our role in speaking the gospel of Christ from a heart of love and a life of service. We have looked at this text repeatedly. But this time our question is different: *What does the reality of the new birth imply for our witness to unbelievers?* Here's a very quick overview of what we have seen in this text (this time without the arguments).

Verse 22: "Having purified your souls by your obedience to the truth for a sincere brotherly love, love one another earnestly from a pure heart." The purification of your soul in verse 22 is what happens in the new birth. The obedience to the truth refers to faith in the gospel. The truth is the gospel of Christ, and obedience to the gospel is faith in Christ.

For a sincere love of the brothers is the outcome and fruit of the new birth. Therefore, Peter says: Now that this has happened to you, "Love one another earnestly from a pure heart." In other words, since you are born again through faith in the gospel with a view to a transformed life of love, now live it out. Love each other.

Then in verse 23 he uses the very language of the new birth: "Since you have been born again, not of perishable seed but of imperishable, through the living and abiding word of God." This is probably the most important verse in the Bible concerning the relationship between the new birth and our role in how it comes about in other people. The key statement is: "You have been born again...through the living and abiding word of God."

In other words, the seed that God uses to create new life in spiritually dead, unbelieving hearts is the seed of the word of God. "You have been born again, not of perishable seed but of imperishable, [that is,] through the living and abiding word of God." There are not many verses in the Bible more important than that. If you see the implications of that, it will change your life profoundly.

WHAT IS THE WORD OF GOD?

But to see the implications, we need to make sure we see what the word of God is. There are different ways to understand the word of God. The world was created by the word of God (Heb. 11:3). Jesus is called the Word of God (John 1:1, 14). The Ten Commandments are called the word of God (Mark 7:13). The promises to Israel are called the word of God (Rom. 9:6).

But here Peter is very specific in what he means in verse 23 by the word of God through which we were born again. First, he says it is living and abiding. "You have been born again... through the living and abiding word of God." The word is living because it has the divine power to give new life. And the word of God is abiding because, once it creates life, it sustains it forever.

Then Peter quotes Isaiah 40:6–8 in verses 24–25 to explain and support this claim about the word of God: "For 'All flesh is like grass and all its glory like the flower of grass. The grass withers, and the flower falls, but the word of the Lord remains forever.'" The word of God is not like grass and flowers. They flourish for a moment and give joy that lasts for a moment. Then they are gone, and the life they sustained is gone. But the word of God is not like that. The life it creates lasts forever because the life-creating and life-sustaining word lasts forever.

Then Peter tells us exactly what he is referring to with this phrase "the word of God." He says in the last part of verse 25, "And this word is the good news that was preached to you." The good news preached to you—that's the imperishable seed; that's the living and abiding word of God through which you were born again. So the way God brings about the new birth in dead, unbelieving hearts is by the gospel, the good news.

THE GREATEST NEWS IN THE WORLD

And the news is this: Christ, the Son of God, died in our place—became our substitute—to pay the price for all our sins, and to accomplish perfect righteousness, and to endure and remove all of God's wrath, and rise from the dead triumphant over death for our eternal life and joy in his presence—and all of this offered freely through faith alone in Jesus Christ alone. That's the good news. To this day, two thousand years later, it remains the greatest news in the world. And there are millions (near and far) who do not know this news.

So here's the point—and it is immensely important if there is anyone you love (or any thousands you love) and want to see born again to a living hope: If people are to be born again, it will happen by hearing the word of God, centered in the gospel of Jesus Christ. They will be "born again through the living and abiding word of God...the gospel." God's work and your work come together like this:

· God causes the new birth through the seed of the word, the gospel.

- God brings about the new birth through your telling people the gospel.
- God regenerates people through the news about who Christ is and what he has done on the cross and in the resurrection.
- God gives new life to dead hearts through your words when you speak the gospel.

GIVING LIFE WITH THE GOSPEL

So, going back to our original question: *What should we be doing to help unbelievers be born again?* Answer: *Tell people the good news of Christ from a heart of love and from a life of service.* We'll say more about the heart of love and the life of service later. But focus here for a moment on this amazing fact: The seed that saves is the word of God—the gospel preached. The seed that creates new life is the gospel in the mouths of believers, spoken to unbelievers. The surgical instrument that opens the eyes of the blind is your words telling and explaining the gospel.

How can this become for us not just a conviction but a passion? I pray that God will use his own word in this chapter to waken this passion. So consider more of his word. James 1:18: "Of his own will he brought us forth by the word of truth." There it is in the words of James, the Lord's brother: "by the word of truth." That was how he brought us forth. And this reference is to the new birth.

In 1 Peter 2:9, just nine verses later than our text in 1:23–25 ("born again through the living and abiding word, the gospel"), Peter says, "You are a chosen race, a royal priesthood, a holy nation, a people for his own possession, that you may proclaim the excellencies of him who called you out of darkness into his marvelous light."

God brought you out of darkness and into his marvelous light by the word of God, the gospel (1:23, 25). And now in this marvelous light what are we to do? Why are we here? One utterly crucial reason while this age remains: "that you may proclaim the excellencies of him who called you out of darkness into his marvelous light." We are in the marvelous light of the love and power and wisdom of Christ so that our joy in that marvelous light might be filled up through proclaiming the excellencies of Christ.

Why? Because that's how others will be born again—by hearing this good news. And when they are born again, they move from darkness to marvelous light and see Christ for who he is, and treasure him for who he is, and therefore magnify him for who he is. And our joy is completed in their joy in him.

WHAT WILL IT TAKE TODAY?

What will it take so that thousands of Christians in our churches become passionate about telling the gospel to unbelievers? One of the reasons we don't do it as much as we should is that life in America is so entertaining that thoughts about desperate, eternal, spiritual need are hard for us to feel, let alone talk about. The world is just too interesting and entertaining. It feels awkward to make ourselves or others uncomfortable with thoughts about perishing people. It's heavy. But life in America is light.

So perhaps what God will choose to do is what he did for the church in Jerusalem. They were not moving out from Jerusalem to Judea, Samaria, and the uttermost parts of the world in evangelism the way Jesus told them to in Acts 1:8. So Stephen was raised up to bear such irresistible testimony (Acts 6:10) that the only way his adversaries could handle him was to kill him (Acts 7:60).

And when they did, the persecution spilled over onto all the Christians in Jerusalem. "And there arose on that day a great persecution against the church in Jerusalem, and they were all scattered throughout the regions of Judea and Samaria, except the apostles" (Acts 8:1). And what was the result? Acts 8:4: "Now those who were scattered went about preaching the word" (Acts 8:4). Literally: "Those who were scattered went about gospelling the word (*euangelizomenoi ton logon*, Acts 8:4–5). They weren't preachers. They were just ordinary folks, thousands of them (Acts 2:41). After they were driven out of their homes, they went everywhere telling the good news.

Is this not an amazing response to persecutions and pain and loss and exile and homelessness? They did not go everywhere complaining. They did not go everywhere questioning God. They went everywhere "telling the good news." O that we would so love the gospel and have so much compassion for lost people that tribulation and distress and persecution and famine and nakedness and danger and sword and gun and terrorist would turn us not into fearful complainers, but bold heralds of good news.

Precisely when they were persecuted, they went everywhere telling the good news of Christ. Maybe the Lord will do it that way. He certainly is doing it that way in some parts of the world, and millions are being born again—through the loving, bold, clear telling of the gospel by persecuted Christians.

DESIRE THE WORD OF GOD

How can we move toward that kind of joyful courage? I will deal with some concrete examples and methods in the final chapter. But I close this chapter by answering this way: We will move toward joyful, bold, gospel-telling when we follow the context of 1 Peter 1:23–25 into the very next verses where Peter gives us this counsel:

> So put away all malice and all deceit and hypocrisy and envy and all slander. Like newborn infants, long for

the pure spiritual milk, that by it you may grow up to salvation—if indeed you have tasted that the Lord is good. (1 Pet. 2:1–3)

This reference to "newborn infants" does not mean that all the saints in that region were immature. They weren't. He is not describing the immature. He is describing what all born-again people desire, and he's encouraging us to desire it the way babies desire milk. And he defines what we should desire as *pure and spiritual*. The word translated *spiritual* (*logikon*) means *spiritual* not in contrast to *carnal* or *fleshly* or *worldly*, but rather in contrast to *literal*. The word here means *symbolic* and, specifically, symbolic of the word of God. So the King James Version is right to translate it *sincere milk of the word*. "Desire the sincere milk of the word" (1 Pet. 2:2).

The point is this: He has just told us that we were born again by the living and abiding word of God, the gospel. Now he says: Desire this every day the way babies desire milk. Feel the need for this every day the way babies must have milk to grow into life, or else they die. "Man does not live by bread alone, but by every word that comes from the mouth of God" (Matt. 4:4).

Peter is saying: If you are going to be free from malice and deceit and hypocrisy and envy and slander—if you are going to tell the gospel from a heart of love and a life of service—then you must hunger and thirst for the word of God the way babies hunger and thirst for milk.

GETTING DRUNK ON THE WORD OF GOD

And why would you want to do this? 1 Peter 2:3 says you will have this desire "if indeed you have tasted that the Lord is good." This is key to personal evangelism: Have you tasted the word of God—especially the gospel—that the Lord is good? Have you tasted it? I am not asking: Have you thought about it? I am not asking: Have you decided to affirm it? I am asking: Have you *tasted* it? Are there living, spiritual taste buds in your heart that taste Christ as more desirable than all else?

This is where we need to get serious. We will spread the seed of God's mighty regenerating power if we have tasted that the Lord is good. The Lord is our delight. The Lord is our Treasure. The Lord is our meat and milk and water and wine. This tasting happens through the word of God. May God loosen our tongues and make us bold gospel-tellers because we are drunk with the wine of the word of God and the goodness of the Lord.

Therefore, having this ministry by the mercy of God, we do not lose heart. But we have renounced disgraceful, underhanded ways. We refuse to practice cunning or to tamper with God's word, but by the open statement of the truth we would commend ourselves to everyone's conscience in the sight of God. And even if our gospel is veiled, it is veiled only to those who are perishing. In their case the god of this world has blinded the minds of the unbelievers, to keep them from seeing the light of the gospel of the glory of Christ, who is the image of God. For what we proclaim is not ourselves, but Jesus Christ as Lord, with ourselves as your servants for Jesus' sake. For God, who said, "Let light shine out of darkness," has shone in our hearts to give the light of the knowledge of the glory of God in the face of Jesus Christ. But we have this treasure in jars of clay, to show that the surpassing power belongs to God and not to us.

2 Corinthians 4:1–7

15

I Am Sending You
to Open Their Eyes

We're ending this book on the ground. On the street. In the car. At Starbucks. In the back yard. In school. At work. Over lunch. On the phone. On Facebook and MySpace. And text messaging. And Skyping. And blogging. And airplanes. And a hundred ordinary conversations. We're ending with personal evangelism—an old-fashioned commitment in new contexts for the sake of the new birth in thousands of spiritually dead people for the glory of Jesus Christ.

We have affirmed repeatedly the biblical truth of 1 Peter 1:23, "You have been born again…through the living and abiding word of God"—followed by the explanation in verse 25: "This word is the good news that was preached to you." In other words, God brings about the new birth through the gospel—the good news that God sent his Son into the world to live a perfect life, die for sinners, absorb the wrath of God, take away our guilt, provide the gift of righteousness, and give eternal joy in Christ through faith alone apart from works of the law.

People are born again through hearing that news, and never born again without it. "Faith comes from hearing, and hearing through the word of Christ" (Rom. 10:17). So when we asked, *What should we do to help people be born again?* the biblical answer was plain: Tell people the good news from a heart of love and a life of service.

In this final chapter, the aim is to underline that main point with a couple of new texts and then give some encouragements and practical helps.

God Makes Light Shine in Our Hearts

2 Corinthians 4:4 pinpoints the condition people are in without Christ. Verse 4: "In their case the god of this world has blinded the minds of the unbelievers, to keep them from seeing the light of the gospel of the glory of Christ, who is the image of God." People who don't believe in Christ are blind. They can't see Christ as supremely valuable, and so they won't receive him as their Treasure and so they are not saved. A work of God is needed in their lives to open their eyes and give them life so they can see and receive Christ as Savior and Lord and Treasure of their lives. That work of God is called the new birth.

Then look at the solution to this condition of blindness and perishing. Verse 6: "For God, who said, 'Let light shine out of darkness,' has shone in our hearts to give the light of the knowledge of the glory of God in the face of Jesus Christ." This is a description of the new birth, even though that term is not used. The God who created light in the beginning does the same thing in the human heart. Only this time, the light is not physical light, but "the light of the knowledge of the glory of God in the face of Christ." Or as verse 4 calls it: "the light of the gospel of the glory of Christ, who is the image of God."

He causes the human heart to see the truth and beauty and worth of Christ—the glory of Christ. And when we see him for who he really is, we receive him for who he is. And to as many as received him, he gave power to become the children of God (John 1:12). That's what we want for our children—at six or sixteen or twenty-six—and for our parents and our spouses and our neighbors and colleagues and our friends at school. We want the light to shine in their hearts so they see and receive Christ. We want them to be born again.

GOD SENDS YOU TO OPEN THEIR EYES

Look at the human means God uses to make this happen. 2 Corinthians 4:5: "What we proclaim is not ourselves, but Jesus Christ as Lord, with ourselves as your servants for Jesus' sake." Paul's role was to proclaim Christ from a heart of love and a life of service. That proclamation is called *the gospel* in verse 3: "Even if our gospel is veiled, it is veiled only to those who are perishing." It's the gospel that spiritually blind people can't see and spiritually deaf people can't hear. So our answer to the question *What should we do to help people be born again?* is: Tell them the good news of Christ from a heart of love and a life of service.

Here is an astonishing picture of human agency in the new birth. In Acts 26, Paul is telling King Agrippa about his conversion and his call to the ministry. He reports the spectacular encounter with Christ on the Damascus Road. Then he reports the commission that Christ gave him. The words of the commission are amazing. Paul says that Jesus told him;

> I am Jesus whom you are persecuting. But rise and stand upon your feet, for I have appeared to you for this purpose, to appoint you as a servant and witness to the things in

> which you have seen me and to those in which I will appear
> to you, delivering you from your people and from the
> Gentiles—to whom I am sending you to open their eyes,
> so that they may turn from darkness to light and from the
> power of Satan to God, that they may receive forgiveness
> of sins and a place among those who are sanctified by faith
> in me. (Acts 26:15–18)

This commission is breathtaking in what it implies about the
role of human beings in the miraculous work of the new birth.
Jesus says to Paul, "I am sending you to open their eyes." And
look what hangs on this mission: "...so that they may turn from
darkness to light and from the power of Satan to God, that they
may receive forgiveness of sins and a place among those who are
sanctified by faith in me."

According to 2 Corinthians 4, people are spiritually blind until
God gives them eyes to see, that is, until God causes them to be
born again. And in Acts 26, Jesus says in verse 18, "I am sending
you to open their eyes." The point is not hard to see. God opens
the eyes of the blind to see the truth and beauty and worth of
Christ. And he does this by sending people to tell the good news
from hearts of love and lives of service.

That is what I find myself praying for more and more. Lord,
fill your church with a passion to open the eyes of the blind. Fill
us with a passion to do what God promises to do by making us a
means of bringing about the new birth. I speak it to you the way
that Jesus spoke it to Paul: Go out and open their eyes.

Don't stop because you can't do this. Of course you can't.
Only God can open the eyes of the blind (2 Cor. 4:6). But the
fact that you can't make electricity or create light never stops you
from flipping light switches. The fact that you can't create fire
in cylinders never stops you from turning the car key. The fact
that you can't create cell tissue never stops you from eating your

meals. So don't let the fact that you can't cause the new birth stop you from telling the gospel. That is how people are born again—through the living and abiding word, the good news of Jesus Christ.

TEN ENCOURAGEMENTS FOR GOSPEL-TELLING

So here are a few encouragements that I hope will help you.

1. *Know This: God Uses Clay Pots*

Back to the context of 2 Corinthians 4:4–6. The next verse is crucial. We don't usually read it in context. Verse 6 has just said that the God who created light in the universe does the same kind of thing in the hearts of blind sinners like us. He gives the "light of the knowledge of the glory of God in the face of Christ." In verse 4, this light is called the "light of the gospel of the glory of Christ."

That's the context. Now here's verse 7: "But we have this treasure in jars of clay, to show that the surpassing power belongs to God and not to us." We have "this treasure." What treasure? "The knowledge of the glory of God in the face of Christ." Or, "the light of the gospel of the glory of Christ." In short: We have the gospel with its light-giving power.

Now the encouragement is this: "We have this treasure in jars of clay." Jars of clay is a reference to us. We are the jars of clay. Compared to the treasure that is in us, we are clay. We are not gold. The gospel is gold. We are not silver. The news about Christ is silver. We are not bronze. The power of Christ is bronze.

This means that if you feel average or below average in your fitness to share the gospel treasure, you are closer to the truth than someone who feels powerful and wise and self-sufficient. Paul wants us to realize that we are clay pots. Not gold or silver or bronze. He wants us to realize that from the most sophisticated to the most average, we are all clay pots when it comes to containing and sharing the gospel. It is so valuable and so powerful that any thought of its container being something comparable is foolish.

How does Paul talk about himself and Apollos, two of the most fruitful Christians in the first century? "What then is Apollos? What is Paul? Servants through whom you believed, as the Lord assigned to each. I planted, Apollos watered, but God gave the growth. So neither he who plants nor he who waters is anything, but only God who gives the growth" (1 Cor. 3:5–7).

What's the point of being a clay pot? Back to 2 Corinthians 4:7: "We have this treasure in jars of clay, to show that the surpassing power belongs to God and not to us." God's aim is that his own power through the gospel, not ours, be exalted. Which means that if you feel average or less than average in your sense of fitness to tell the gospel, you are the person God is looking for—a clay pot, who simply shares the treasure of the gospel, not the glitzy intellect, not the glitzy eloquence, not the glitzy beauty or strength or cultural cleverness. Then God will do his work through the gospel, and the surpassing power will belong to him and not to us.

Be encouraged, ordinary Christian. You are appointed, precisely in your ordinariness, for the greatest work in the world: opening the eyes of the blind and showing the Treasure of Christ.

2. *Get Resources to Share*

Giving away good Christian literature is one way of extending your personal witness about the gospel. At *www.desiringGod.org* we try to make evangelistic booklets available as inexpensively as possible or for whatever price you can afford.[23] There are dozens of other very useful materials available.

The point is: Think this way. Think: Wherever I can, I want to commend Christ. I want to tell the story that God uses to give people life. Put something in your pocket, your purse, your briefcase, your car. And pray every day, Lord, make me an instrument of gospel-spreading today. Use me to open the eyes of the blind.

3. *Know that God May Use Many Influences*

Keep in mind that what you say to someone about Jesus may be supplemented by a half dozen others that God is providentially lining up to speak to this person as God pursues him for salvation. You may feel your word was wasted. It is never wasted (1 Cor. 15:58). Your word may be the beginning of the influences. Or it may be the final, decisive word that God uses to bring a person to faith. Speak your word. The smallest word about Christ is not wasted.

A young woman told the story as she was joining our church of how Christ saved her. She said that she knew a good bit about Christianity because of her parents but had thrown it all away as a teenager and was on her own. One day she and her friends were walking down the beach as several handsome guys approached. Her thought was to impress them and be thought attractive and cool. As the guys passed, one of them called out, "Praise Jesus!"

Now probably later that night those guys said to themselves, "That was a lame witness. Why didn't we stop and talk?" Little did they know that this simple word, "Praise Jesus," pierced her

23 Two examples would be the booklet *For Your Joy* and the tract *The Quest for Joy.*

heart and sent her later to her knees and to the Savior. There are no wasted testimonies.

4. Be a Lavish Giver

Be known as a generous person, not a stingy person. Jesus said, "Lend, expecting nothing in return" (Luke 6:35). I mean this in general about all that you own. Stingy people make Jesus look unimportant and unsatisfying. But more specifically I mean: Be lavish in your giving of good books—if you know unbelievers who are readers. Give a Christian book that cost you ten or fifteen or thirty dollars. Offer it as a gift and tell them what it meant to you and that you would love to talk about it some time. If you don't know the person, ask for their permission to give them a book that meant a lot to you.

This is what I regularly do on the plane. Sometimes conversations are easy to get into about Christ because I am a pastor. Other times they're not. But in either case, I often say, "I wrote a book that I would love to give to you. May I give you one?" People almost never say no. I put different books in my briefcase to give away. The most common ones are *Seeing and Savoring Jesus Christ*, *Fifty Reasons Why Jesus Came to Die*, *Desiring God*, and *When the Darkness Will Not Lift*. I also keep some of these in the drawer by our front door at home in case there is an opportunity to give one to someone at the door. Choose a few short books that you have read that have helped your faith, and keep a stash of them in key places. Develop the habit of thinking this way: How can I commend Christ today? Be lavish in your giving.

And, of course, give away the Bible. I happened to open a biography of the missionary Henry Martyn recently and read this about the author, B. V. Henry: "Henry came to personal faith in Christ at the age of 17 through reading a New Testament given to him by an elderly lady."[24] Be lavish in giving away Bibles and portions of the Bible.[25]

5. *Find People Interesting*

Be encouraged that simply finding people interesting and caring about them is a beautiful pathway into their heart. Evangelism gets a bad reputation when we are not really interested in people and don't seem to care about them. People really are interesting. Every person you talk to is an amazing creation of God with a thousand interesting experiences. Remember the words of C. S. Lewis:

> It is a serious thing to live in a society of possible gods and goddesses, to remember that the dullest and most uninteresting person you talk to may one day be a creature which, if you saw it now, you would strongly be tempted to worship, or else a horror and a corruption such as you now meet, if at all, only in a nightmare. All day long we are, in some degree, helping each other to one or other of these destinations. It is in the light of these overwhelming possibilities, it is with the awe and the circumspection proper to them, that we should conduct all our dealings with one another, all friendships, all loves, all play, all politics. There are no ordinary people. You have never talked to a mere mortal.[26]

Yet, most of us don't think this way. The gods bore us, and we return to our video games. Very few people are interested in others. If you really find their story interesting, and care about them, they may open up to you and want to hear your story—Christ's story.

24 B. V. Henry, *Forsaking All for Christ: A Biography of Henry Martyn* (London: Chapter Two, 2003), 167.

25 You can buy the entire Bible in the *English Standard Version* at Desiring God for under $4.00. http://www.desiringgod.org/store/topicindex/54/720_ESV_Paperback_Bible_Outreach_Edition/

26 C. S. Lewis, *The Weight of Glory* (Grand Rapids, MI: Eerdmans, 1949), 14–15.

6. *Invite People to Church*

In your relationships, invite people to church even before they are Christians. Some of the sheer strangeness of what it means to be a Christian can be overcome by a growing familiarity with how we sing and talk and relate in church. And the preaching of the word of God has a unique power. Every kind of speech is unique in some way. Preaching is not the only or the main way that we communicate. But it is appointed by God for a special effectiveness. "After that in the wisdom of God the world by wisdom knew not God, it pleased God *by the foolishness of preaching* to save them that believe" (1 Cor. 1:21 KJV). Or, nowadays, with the Internet, if they are hesitant to come to church, invite them to a website where they can watch or listen to your pastor or some other teacher.

7. *Fill the City with Gospel Teaching*

When the apostles were put on trial in Jerusalem, the high priest said, "You have filled Jerusalem with your teaching" (Acts 5:28). That is what I dream for the churches of my city. If all the Christians were talking about Christ, and giving out literature about Christ, and sending emails about Christ, and inviting people to church for Christ, and being lavishly generous to others for Christ, then someone might say, "Those Christians have filled the city with their teaching." May it be so.

8. *Use Your Giftings*

Be encouraged that we all have different gifts and should not try to imitate everything about anyone. Every Christian should be a servant (Gal. 5:13), but some have a gift of service (Rom. 12:7). Every Christian should have a heart of mercy (Luke 6:36), but some have a gift of mercy (Rom. 12:8). Every Christian should speak to others about Christ (1 Pet. 2:9), but some have a gift of prophecy and exhortation and teaching (Rom. 12:7).

The point is: We are all in this together, but some are gifted one way and some another. Find where you fit, and stoke the flames of your effectiveness there. Grow in every area, but don't paralyze yourself because you are not like someone else. God made you and means to use you—the unique you—in evangelism.

9. Read Books on Evangelism

Here are two older books and one newer one: Will Metzger's *Tell the Truth*; J. I. Packer's *Evangelism and the Sovereignty of God*; and Mark Dever's *The Gospel and Personal Evangelism*.[27] There are, of course, dozens of books worthy of your attention. My point is simply to encourage you to think this way—to include in your mindset the desire to be instructed and inspired by what others have written on personal evangelism.

10. Pray for Boldness

It is remarkable to notice that most of the prayers relating to evangelism in the New Testament relate to prayers for the gospel-tellers, not the gospel-hearers. Romans 10:1 is an exception to that: "Brothers, my heart's desire and prayer to God for them is that they may be saved." But mostly we read things like "Pray for us, that the word of the Lord may speed ahead and be honored" (2 Thess. 3:1). "Pray also for us, that God may open to us a door for the word, to declare the mystery of Christ" (Col. 4:3). "Keep alert with all perseverance, making supplication for...me, that

27 Metzger, *Tell the Truth: Whole Gospel to the Whole Person by the Whole People*, third ed. (Downers Grove, IL: InterVarsity Press, 202, orgi 1981); Packer, *Evangelism and the Sovereignty of God* (Downers Grove, IL: InterVarsity Press, 2009, orig. 1961); Dever, *The Gospel and Personal Evangelism* (Wheaton, IL: Crossway Books, 2007).

words may be given to me in opening my mouth boldly to proclaim the mystery of the gospel" (Eph. 6:18–19).

Pray for yourself and your family and your church and your pastors in these ways. It is remarkable and encouraging that the apostle Paul felt the need to ask the churches to pray for his boldness. If Paul needed those prayers, how much more do you and I.

Speaking the Word of God with Boldness

Make Acts 4:31 your dream and prayer for the church of Christ: "When they had prayed, the place in which they were gathered together was shaken, and they were all filled with the Holy Spirit and continued to speak the word of God with boldness." If God would have mercy on us and pour out the Holy Spirit in this way on his church, our eyes would be bright with bold joy and our mouths would open with the story of the gospel. We would become a people who look and sound like we have heard the greatest news in the world—which we have. That is how we were born again. And that is how others will be born again.

You have been born again...
through the living and abiding word of God...
And this word is the good news.

1 Peter 1:23–25

Conclusion

The New Birth
and the New World

Jesus' words "You must be born again" (John 3:7) go to the heart of the world's problems. There will be no final peace, no final justice, no triumph over hate and selfishness and racism without this profound change in human nature.

All other diagnoses and remedies are superficial. They may even be valuable—like laws that restrain people from doing their worst. But without the new birth, people are not changed at the root, and that is where the problem lies. If human beings are not changed at the root, then our innate selfishness will spoil every dream.

Jesus' remedy fits the depths of our disorder. If we only did bad things because of bad circumstances, then there might be hope that changing the circumstances would change our behavior. But our problem is not simply that we do bad things— like slandering others, and cheating in private, and neglecting our responsibilities, and shunning those who are different, and doing shoddy work, and bending the truth, and gratifying our desires at others' expense, and ignoring the poor, and giving no regard to our Maker.

Our problem is that what we do comes from who we are. "Are grapes gathered from thornbushes, or figs from thistles? So, every healthy tree bears good fruit, but the diseased tree bears bad fruit" (Matt. 7:16–17). "Out of the abundance of the heart the mouth speaks" (Matt. 12:34). That's Jesus' explanation of why human beings bear bad fruit. It's not that there's been a drought. No, the tree is diseased.

Jesus' radical remedy will never make sense until we own up to his diagnosis of our condition. The human heart is innately selfish. Jesus had no romantic notions about the best of men. He loved his disciples. He knew they were kind fathers. But he matter-of-factly called them evil. "If you then, who are evil, know how to give good gifts to your children..." (Matt. 7:11). He agreed with the prophet Jeremiah, "The heart is more deceitful than all else and is desperately sick; who can understand it?" (Jer. 17:9).

Jesus would have approved of the apostle Paul's penetrating description of the layers of our corruption. Humans suffer from "the futility of their minds, being darkened in their understanding, excluded from the life of God because of the ignorance that is in them, because of the hardness of their heart" (Eph. 4:17–18). At the bottom of our wills—at the root, at the spring—we are hard. There are no exceptions. "For in your sight no man living is righteous" (Ps. 143:2).

Jesus' remedy for this was and is "You must be born again." He put everything in place to make it possible. He lived a sinless life. He died for our sins. He endured the wrath of God in our place. He paid the penalty for our transgressions. He purchased eternal life. He secured all the promises of God. He rose from the dead. He conquered death and hell and Satan. He reigns at God's right hand and intercedes for us. He will come again to "make his blessings flow far as the curse is found." He did all of that to make the gift of the new birth possible. All those blessings are sure for those who are born again.

The connection between those blessings and us is the new birth. That is Jesus' root remedy for our depravity. Personal and social and global renewal will not be possible without this most fundamental of all changes. It is the root of all true and lasting change.

Someone may say: "I know religious people—Christian, Jewish, Muslim, Hindu, Buddhist, cultic—who act like vipers. They aren't part of the renewal." Jesus knew them too. But he did not infer from this that the new birth doesn't work. He infers that they are hypocrites. "You clean the outside of the cup and the plate, but inside they are full of greed and self-indulgence" (Matt. 23:25). "You are like whitewashed tombs, which outwardly appear beautiful, but within are full of dead people's bones" (Matt. 23:27).

Religious fakes were no surprise to Jesus. He prepared his most stinging words for them. They do not contradict the new birth. They confirm it. What could possibly change a "brood of vipers" (Matt. 12:34)? Reformation is not what vipers need. They need regeneration. Religious fraud does not make the new birth nonsense; it makes it necessary.

So if your heartache is for your own personal change, or for change in your marriage, or change in your prodigal children, or in your church, or in the systemic structures of injustice, or in the political system, or in the hostilities among nations, or in the human degradation of the environment, or in the raunchiness of our entertainment culture, or in the miseries of the poor, or in the callous opulence of the rich, or in the inequities of educational opportunity, or in arrogant attitudes of ethnocentrism, or in a hundred areas of human need caused by some form of human greed—if your heart aches for any of these, then you should care supremely about the new birth.

There are other ways of shaping culture and guiding behavior. But none so deep. None so far-reaching. None so universally relevant. None so eternally significant.

Someday, at the return of the Lord Jesus, the world will be made new. The kingdom of God will come fully. Jesus himself will be the great all-satisfying Treasure in that new and beautiful earth. But not everyone will enjoy it. "Truly, truly," Jesus said, "unless one is born again he cannot see the kingdom of God" (John 3:3). Jesus is the way, the truth, and the life (John 14:6). Until we come to him, we will not have life. Not now. Not ever. God gives eternal life, and this life is in his Son (1 John 5:11). Whoever has the Son has life (1 John 5:12). His word is reliable: "Come to me that you may have life" (John 5:40). If you come, you will be truly, invincibly, finally alive.

Scripture Index

Persons Index

Subject Index

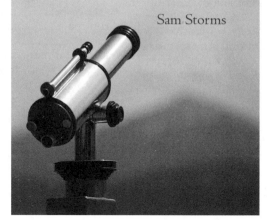

'The more I ponder the source and ground of all our lasting joy, the more convinced I become that Sam Storms is right. It's the Beauty of God.'

John Piper

onething

Developing a Passion
for the Beauty of God

Sam Storms

One Thing:

Developing a passion for the beauty of God

Sam Storms

The goal of our creation was not simply that we might be happy, but happy in appreciating God's own glory. We were made to glorify God and enjoy him forever. Nothing is more important than understanding this truth. This inspiring work helps us see that beauty has the power to convince the inquiring mind of truth. The soul's contact with God's beauty elicits love and forges in us a new affection that no earthly power can overcome. Enjoying God in the revelation of his beauty is the solution to our struggle with sin, the catalyst for substantive and lasting change and is the soul's satisfaction, with which no rival pleasure can hope to compete.

So what is it about God that when known, seen and experienced empowers the human soul to feel sickened in the presence of sin and satisfied in the divine embrace? That word again: Beauty.

Apatheism affects not just those outside the church but those inside the church who can't be bothered with their own religion let alone someone else's.

> The more I ponder the source and ground of all our lasting joy, the more convinced I become that Sam Storms is right. It's the Beauty of God. In all his gifts we are to see him. Especially in the gospel.... Let Sam Storms guide you biblically and waken your heart to the Treasure of Christ who is the image of the Beauty of God.
>
> John Piper

Sam Storms is Pastor of Bridgeway Church, Oklahoma City, Oklahoma and founder of Enjoying God Ministries.

ISBN 978-1-85792-952-2

❊ desiringGod

If you would like to further explore the vision of God and life presented in this book, we at Desiring God would love to serve you. We have hundreds of resources to help you grow in your passion for Jesus Christ and help you spread that passion to others. At our website, desiringGod.org, you'll find almost every-thing John Piper has written and preached, including more than thirty books. We've made over twenty-five years of his sermons available free online for you to read, listen to, download, and in some cases watch.

In addition, you can access hundreds of articles, find out where John Piper is speaking, learn about our conferences, dis-cover our God-centered children's curricula, and browse our online store. John Piper receives no royalties from the books he writes and no compensation from Desiring God. The funds are all reinvested into our gospel-spreading efforts. Desiring God also has a what-ever-you-can-afford policy, designed for individuals with limited discretionary funds. If you'd like more information about this policy, please contact us at the address or phone number below. We exist to help you treasure Jesus Christ and his gospel above all things because he is most glorified in you when you are most satisfied in him. Let us know how we can serve you!

Desiring God
Post Office Box 2901
Minneapolis, Minnesota 55402
888.346.4700   mail@desiringGog

Christian Focus Publications

publishes books for all ages
Our mission statement –

STAYING FAITHFUL

In dependence upon God we seek to help make His infallible Word, the Bible, relevant. Our aim is to ensure that the Lord Jesus Christ is presented as the only hope to obtain forgiveness of sin, live a useful life and look forward to heaven with Him.

REACHING OUT

Christ's last command requires us to reach out to our world with His gospel. We seek to help fulfil that by publishing books that point people towards Jesus and help them develop a Christ-like maturity. We aim to equip all levels of readers for life, work, ministry and mission.

Books in our adult range are published in three imprints.

Christian Focus contains popular works including biographies, commentaries, basic doctrine and Christian living. Our children's books are also published in this imprint.

Mentor focuses on books written at a level suitable for Bible College and seminary students, pastors, and other serious readers. The imprint includes commentaries, doctrinal studies, examination of current issues and church history.

Christian Heritage contains classic writings from the past.

Christian Focus Publications Ltd
Geanies House, Fearn, Ross-shire,
IV20 1TW, Scotland, United Kingdom
info@christianfocus.com
www.christianfocus.com